CAMBRIDGE LIBRARY COLLECTION

Books of enduring scholarly value

Archaeology

The discovery of material remains from the recent or the ancient past has always been a source of fascination, but the development of archaeology as an academic discipline which interpreted such finds is relatively recent. It was the work of Winckelmann at Pompeii in the 1760s which first revealed the potential of systematic excavation to scholars and the wider public. Pioneering figures of the nineteenth century such as Schliemann, Layard and Petrie transformed archaeology from a search for ancient artifacts, by means as crude as using gunpowder to break into a tomb, to a science which drew from a wide range of disciplines - ancient languages and literature, geology, chemistry, social history - to increase our understanding of human life and society in the remote past.

Northern 'Ajlûn

Gottlieb Schumacher (1857–1925) was an American-born German civil engineer, architect and archaeologist who was influential in the early archaeological explorations of Palestine. His parents were members of the Temple Association, a Protestant group who emigrated to Haifa in 1869. After studying engineering in Stuttgart between 1876 and 1881, Schumacher returned to Haifa and soon assumed a leading role in surveying and construction in the region. First published in 1890 for the Palestine Exploration Fund, this volume contains the results of Schumacher's survey of Northern 'Aljûn in present-day Jordan. This region contains the ancient Decapolis, a group of ten Hellenistic cities which were centres of Greek and Roman culture. Schumacher describes the contemporary villages and ancient ruins in this area, and includes the results of the first surveys of the Decapolis cities of Gadara and Arbela, and the disputed site of Capitolias.

Cambridge University Press has long been a pioneer in the reissuing of out-of-print titles from its own backlist, producing digital reprints of books that are still sought after by scholars and students but could not be reprinted economically using traditional technology. The Cambridge Library Collection extends this activity to a wider range of books which are still of importance to researchers and professionals, either for the source material they contain, or as landmarks in the history of their academic discipline.

Drawing from the world-renowned collections in the Cambridge University Library, and guided by the advice of experts in each subject area, Cambridge University Press is using state-of-the-art scanning machines in its own Printing House to capture the content of each book selected for inclusion. The files are processed to give a consistently clear, crisp image, and the books finished to the high quality standard for which the Press is recognised around the world. The latest print-on-demand technology ensures that the books will remain available indefinitely, and that orders for single or multiple copies can quickly be supplied.

The Cambridge Library Collection will bring back to life books of enduring scholarly value (including out-of-copyright works originally issued by other publishers) across a wide range of disciplines in the humanities and social sciences and in science and technology.

Northern 'Ajlûn

'Within the Decapolis'

GOTTLIEB SCHUMACHER

CAMBRIDGE
UNIVERSITY PRESS

CAMBRIDGE UNIVERSITY PRESS

Cambridge, New York, Melbourne, Madrid, Cape Town, Singapore,
São Paolo, Delhi, Dubai, Tokyo

Published in the United States of America by Cambridge University Press, New York

www.cambridge.org
Information on this title: www.cambridge.org/9781108017572

© in this compilation Cambridge University Press 2010

This edition first published 1890
This digitally printed version 2010

ISBN 978-1-108-01757-2 Paperback

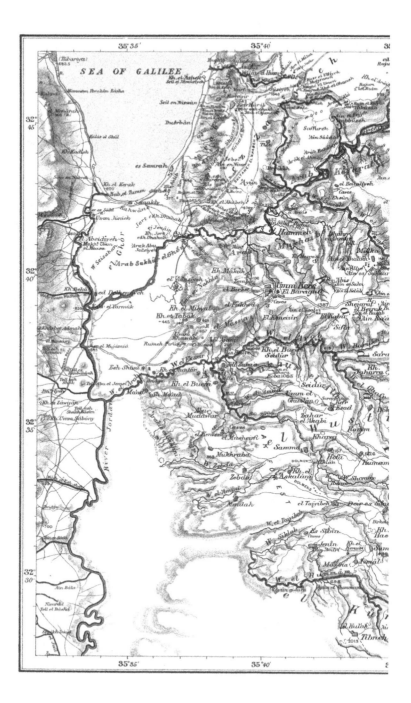

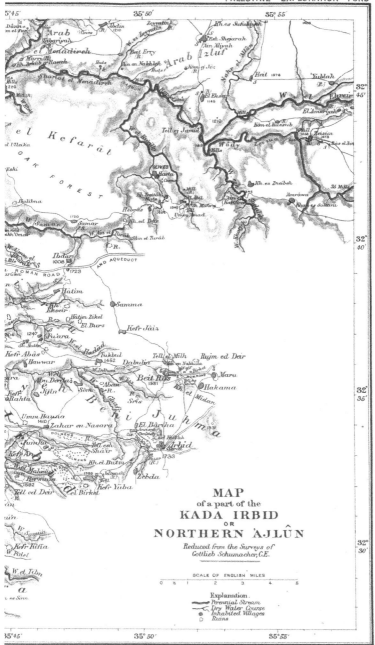

MAP
of a part of the
KADA IRBID
OR
NORTHERN AJLÛN

Reduced from the Surveys of
Gottlieb Schumacher, C.E.

SCALE OF ENGLISH MILES

0   ½   1   2   3   4   5

Explanation.
Perennial Stream
Dry Water Course
Inhabited Villages
Ruins

Stanford's Geog.l Estab.t London

PALESTINE EXPLORATION FUND.

NORTHERN 'AJLÛN,

"WITHIN THE DECAPOLIS."

BY

GOTTLIEB SCHUMACHER, C.E.

Published for the Committee of the Palestine Exploration Fund.

LONDON:
ALEXANDER P. WATT.

1890.

LONDON :
HARRISON AND SONS, ST. MARTIN'S LANE,
PRINTERS IN ORDINARY TO HER MAJESTY.

PREFATORY NOTE.

———◆———

AT the request of the Committee of the Palestine Exploration Fund I have undertaken to prepare Herr Schumacher's present Memoir for the press, and effect such alterations in the English as were needful to make his descriptions comprehensible. The present Map and Memoir deal with a most important tract of country—namely, the ancient Decapolis of Peræa—and besides very numerous sites, still showing ancient remains, the Greek or Roman names of which have been utterly lost, plans and drawings have now been made of the important ruins of Gadara (Umm Keis), Capitolias (Beit Râs), and Arbela (Irbid), none of which had ever before been surveyed. Herr Schumacher also met with two new fields of Dolmens, both covering a considerable extent of ground, and consisting of many hundreds of these monuments. The greater number of specimens, in one of the fields, lay still undisturbed, and the examination of their contents proved that in some instances at least Dolmens in Palestine were used as places of sepulture.

It is to be regretted that no inscriptions were found among the ruins examined during the present survey ; the explanation is probably to be sought in the friable nature of the material (crumbling lime-stone) of which the buildings in northern 'Ajlûn are constructed, and the weathered condition of most of the stones.

The Arabic text of the names is given in the Index, and in this I have copied the list, with the "significations" sent in by Herr Schumacher. These are written in the modern Arab dialect of Palestine, which differs both in orthography and etymology from the classical language of the Arabic dictionaries.

GUY LE STRANGE.

CONTENTS.

———◆———

LIST OF ILLUSTRATIONS.

———◆———

INTRODUCTION.

——◆——

DURING the course of a railway survey, carried
over the high plateaus of Haurân and Jaulân, I
found occasion to extend my researches into the
neighbouring Kada of Irbid, the country sometimes called 'Ajlûn, which includes part of the
Biblical district of the Decapolis or Ten Cities.
This district lies on the south or left bank of the
Yarmûk, which river formed the southern limits of
the Map which accompanied the Memoir published
in 1886 under the title of "Across the Jordan." *
During my journeys through 'Ajlûn, special attention was directed to the Wâd el-'Arab and its
tributaries, for it was originally my intention to
have extended the surveys eastwards as far as the
Wâd esh-Shelâleh. I found, however, that this

———

* "Across the Jordan" being an exploration and survey
of a part of Haurân and Jaulân, by G. Schumacher,
published by the Fund, 1886.

country was so intersected with ravines and wâdies, covered by a thick growth of oak forest, as to render its survey extremely laborious, and the time at my disposal being limited, I was forced to abandon my task, after having mapped and examined only a portion of this interesting country. The sites of Umm Keis, the ancient Gadara, and Beit Râs, the supposed representative of Capitolias, had not hitherto been as thoroughly explored as their importance seemed to merit, and I therefore spent nearly two weeks of my time amidst their ruins, in order to make the detailed plans and sketches which will be found in the following Memoir.

The Map, drawn on the same scale as those already published of Haurân and Jaulân, is based on a trigonometrical survey, made with a theodolite. I adopted as base lines the distance between Tabor and Kaukab el-Hawa (fixed by the Palestine Survey), and that between Tabor and Kefr Hâreb (measured during my late surveys). The chief heights, as those of Umm Keis, Beit Râs, Kefr Esad, Irbid and others, were determined by measuring the angles with the theodolite, and subordinate points were fixed by barometric observations. In regard to archæological researches, I must repeat what I have already written in "Across the Jordan" (pages 241, 292). The real object of my survey, which was to become acquainted with the physical aspect of the country, its people and its products, did not leave me sufficient time to explore the numerous ancient sites with all the care and thoroughness that I should have wished, and in this matter I must throw myself on the indulgence of the reader, hoping that another opportunity may occur for re-visiting the country, which will enable me to continue my explorations and add what may have escaped my notice in the survey which is now laid before the subscribers of the Palestine Exploration Fund.

G. Schumacher.

CHAPTER I.

THE KADA, OR PROVINCE OF IRBID, ITS NAMES, DIVISIONS, AND BOUNDARIES.

THE country described in the following Memoir covers an area of about 220 English square miles, and forms part, politically, of the great Kaimakâmiyeh, or Kada, of Irbid, one of the districts subordinate to the Liva (or Province) of Haurân. It is governed by a Kaimakâm, or Lieutenant-Governor, the subordinate Government Officials and the Mejlis el-Adâra, or Administrative Council, which last is chosen from among the most prominent Sheikhs of the villages in the district. A military force of some 40 mounted soldiers, "Khayyâleh el-Mîreh," and some Zaptiyehs, or Police, are also at the disposal of the Kaimakâm.

The Kada of Irbid is bounded on the north by the Yarmûk River and the country of Jaulân; on the east in part by the Wâd* esh-Shelâleh and the

---

* The final "y" in the word "Wâdy," when it stands before a vowel, is often omitted in the modern dialects. Mr. Schumacher's transcription has in these cases been preserved as giving the present usage.—EDITOR.

Haurân province, in part by the Syrian desert; on the south by the Wâd ez-Zerka and the Belka Province; and on the west by the Ghôr of the Jordan, forming part of the Government of Tabarîyeh (Tiberias Province).

The Kada of Irbid is subdivided into several districts called Nâhiyet (in the plural, in Arabic, called Nawâhy): and the following five Nâhiyets are for the most part included in the map of the country surveyed :—

1. Nâhiyet es-Siru,
2.   „   el-Kefarât,
3.   „   el-Wustîyeh,
4.   „   of the Beni Juhma,
5.   „   el-Kûra.

The southern half of the Kada of Irbid, lying between Tibneh and Kala't 'Ajlûn is called Jebel Ajlûn, and from it the Kada of Irbid is often spoken of as the Kada of 'Ajlûn, a name more often found in the descriptions of European travellers than heard in the mouths of the natives. In order to avoid mistakes it should be clearly understood that the name of Jebel 'Ajlûn is in no case given to those parts of the Kada of Irbid ying *north* of Tibneh (as wrongly printed in Van de Velde's Map, and others), but only to the tract lying between the Wâdy et-Tibn and the Wâd ez-Zerka. The Nâhiyets north of the Wâd et-Tibn up to the Yarmûk, taken collectively, bear no official name, and in calling these " Northern 'Ajlûn" I have been prompted by the wish to make this tract of country (that given in the present Map) familiar to my readers under a single denomination.

General Physical Characteristics.

The geological formation, and, as a consequence, the soil and the general appearance of the Kada Irbid, differs entirely from what is found in Haurân and Jaulân. The rich lava soil of Haurân, formed by the ancient volcanic outbursts of the region of Jaulân, extends but little south of the Yarmûk. According to Dr. Nœtling's Observations ("Zeit der D. Palästina Vereins," Band ix., 1886), the lava streams which took their rise in the high plateau of the Jaulân made their way down the Yarmûk Valley, and after forming two terraces, one in the upper height and the other in the lower along the slopes, finally spread over the Ghôr of the Jordan, near Tâket el-'Elu and El 'Adeisîyeh. With these streams the volcanic region comes to an end, and a less fertile, yellowish-white, calcareous formation follows southwards, and continues over the whole of Northern 'Ajlûn. The rock of this formation is generally a species of crumbling-limestone, and is far inferior for building purposes to the basaltic stone of Haurân. In the Nâhiyets of the Beni Juhma and of El Kûra, a common kind of marble is found. The poor nature of the building stone is probably the cause why the ancient sites of 'Ajlûn are in such a ruinous state, and afford so few remains to reward the search of the explorer; the architectural details also (and for the same reason) are less perfect and less rich than those which meet the eye among the ruins of the Haurân.

The deep valleys of Northern 'Ajlûn are so numerous that the character of the plateau land is almost masked, although the altitudes of the various sections differ but little one from the other, and the rise of the ground level is continuous. The rise is gradual from the west eastwards; from the Ghôr, 700 to 800 feet below the sea, to the plains round Meru and Beit Râs, which lies 1,931 feet above the sea level. In its extension from north to south, the land rises from the Yarmûk River, where it has an average height of a few hundred feet below the surface of the Mediterranean, up towards the narrow shoulder between Umm Keis (+ 1,193 feet) and Ibdar

(+ 1,608 feet), this being the watershed between
the Yarmûk River and the Wâd el-'Arab. From
this point the section shows a remarkable depression running across the wide Wâd el-'Arab, while
further east it remains nearly on a level as far as
the borders of Wâd et-Tibn (+ 1,500 feet). From
here the ground makes a rapid ascent to the high
lands of Tibneh (+ 2,013 feet), which are the
most conspicuous heights on the present Map,
and thence rises again, in regular terraces, which
extend across Jebel 'Ajlûn and on as far as its
southern borders.

The most important depression on the present
Map is formed by the Wâd el-'Arab and its tributaries. This river, which flows in a rapid stream
down a narrow bed between limestone rocks, runs
for the greater part at a level below that of the
Mediterranean. In its winding course from east
to west it forms the main stream of Northern
'Ajlûn, and receives in its bed all the winter torrents which flow down between its northern watershed and the Wâd et-Taiyibeh. The Wâd el-'Arab
is the great water power and reservoir of this part
of 'Ajlûn, for with its tributary, the Wâdy Zahar,
it supplies all the needs of the inhabitants, turning
their mills, and affording them watering and
bathing places. No other valley in this country
can rival it in fertility, for all the other Wâdies

(with the exception of the almost inaccessible Wâdy Samar) run dry in summer, or preserve at most but a few unimportant springs. The inhabitants of other Wâdies, therefore, are generally in lack of good drinking water, and are, as a rule, obliged to provide for their wants from the water found in the more or less filthy cisterns which lie scattered over the length and breadth of the country, and which are a heritage come down to them from their predecessors in possession. The numerous ancient cisterns, and the aqueduct which in old times was built to supply Umm Keis from a great distance with spring water, go to prove that from the earliest epoch this district of the Decapolis was poor in spring water, a feature which finds its explanation geologically in the cleft formation of the rock, of which the country is formed, which is unsuited to collect or retain for any length of time the supplies of water which pour down on the land during the rainy season.

The watershed between the Wâd el-'Arab and the Yarmûk (and the Wâdy Samar) follows a line running from Umm Keis, at 1,200 feet, to a culminating point lying east of Ibdar, at a height of about 1,800 feet above the sea, and forms a narrow shoulder falling abruptly off towards the north and south.   Characteristic of this watershed are the long narrow side spurs (as at Dhahr el-Ahmâr, and elsewhere), which extend northwards down to the Yarmûk Valley, the deep ravines in between showing many curious landslips, as those at 'Arâk el-Heitalîyeh and at other spots. From near Ibdar the watershed continues eastward to near 'Ain et-Turâb, and then follows the range of hills above Beit Râs and on to Irbid, and, trending still further south-east, passes outside the limits of the present Map. On the south, the line of watershed begins near Tell ed-Deir, and runs to Et Taiyibeh, thence follows the road to Samma and Mukhraba, and on down the shoulder of the Ard el-Musheirfi to M'aâd in the west. The water-basin thus comprised occupies about two-thirds of the area of the present Map. The shape of this region is triangular ; broad in the east and narrowing towards the west.

A second line of watershed, that closing off the Wâd et-Taiyibeh and the Wâd el-Hummâm (and Wâd et-Tibn), passes along the shoulder from near Kefr Kifia to Samû'a and along to Es Sibia, running west of Mukhraba, Zebda, and Mendah, where many short ravines run down into the Ghôr, taking their rise near the south-western watershed of Wâd el-'Arab.

The various wâdies on the Map will be described below in their alphabetical order, under each separate Nâhiyet or district.

The soil is, as already stated, generally poor in

Northern 'Ajlûn. Of a superior quality is that of the plain lying west of Umm Keis, which is partly covered with lava remains, as likewise the shoulder running from here eastwards to Ibdar. On the slopes of the Wâd el-'Arab good pasturage is found during the springtide, as well as along the shaded and partly-watered beds of the branch Wâdies, where sufficient food for the cattle and flocks is also met with during the whole of summer. In the eastern region lying between the Wâd el-Ghafr and the before-mentioned shoulder near Ibdar, and bounded by the lands of the Wâd el-'Arab, Beit Râs, El-Bâriha, and Zaher en-Nasâra,—a very stony, unfertile district is found, which in its general aspect resembles the stony region of Jaulân. This track, though now uninhabited, proved on examination to have been thickly settled in ancient times. Eastwards from Kefr Jâiz, Beit Râs, and Irbid, the soil improves, and the wide plain of El-Buk'â, as well as the country round Maru, bears a close resemblance to the excellent soil of the Haurân Province, which begins a few miles east of the limits of the present Map on the further side of the Wâd esh-Shelâleh.

The inhabited villages of Northern 'Ajlûn do not lie very close to one another, and considerable tracts of uncultivated land are met with. A number of the small towns, however, have lands in the

Jordan Valley, where the soil, temperature, and water supply are all that can be desired.

If, however, the general physical characteristics of Northern 'Ajlûn are in many respects inferior to those of the Haurân plateau, the region enjoys an advantage which Haurân totally lacks, namely, in the abundant growth of its oak forests. From Umm Keis eastwards towards Haurân, from the head waters of the Wâd el-'Arab and along the Wâd el-Ghafr southwards to Sôm, Bersînia, and Tibneh (and still further south beyond the limits of the present Map), and westwards, to the slopes of the Ghôr, the entire region is thickly covered with forests of the stone-oak, called *Mallûl*, *Sindiân*, and *Ballût*, in Arabic. These trees, although of the same species, are in their growth far superior to the oaks of Western Palestine or even of Northern Jaulân. The small number of the in- habitants of the country, and the scantiness of the flocks and herds, have up to the present preserved uninjured this fine growth of forest, which is hardly to be matched in any other part of Palestine ; and it is to be hoped that civilisation, which is now making steady progress in 'Ajlûn, will not cause the destruction of these ancient trees.

Along the eastern slopes of the Wâd el-'Arab, especially below Zahan el-'Akabi, also along the Wâd el-'Amûd and the Khallet Abu Lôz, wild

almond trees are abundantly found. According to
the local tradition, they were originally planted in
the "Krûm" or gardens. In the river beds and
on the slopes of most of the wâdies, besides
various kinds of oaks, we find the mock orange
(*Styrax officinalis*), called *Abhar* and *Libna* (لبنة)
in 'Ajlûn ; oleander and cane - brakes occur,
especially near the streams of the wâdy el-
'Arab ; *Kharrub* (St. John's Bread), and *Butm*
(terebinths) cover the northern shoulders of
the Wâdy el-'Arab ; while *Hummud* (sorrel),
the Dôm-tree of the Ghôr, a kind of thorn, here
called *Rubbeida*, and great quantities of *Kubbâr*
(Caper-shrubs), and olive trees are found near the
villages and ruins. The olive trees are generally
very old, and are occasionally called *Rumelli*—
meaning that they are " of the Romans " or Greeks,
who may possibly have originally planted them ;
for the present generation of Arabs certainly does
not occupy itself with the cultivation of these trees.
The numerous oil-presses found scattered about
the forest lands and near the villages prove that
the olive culture was once in a very flourishing
state throughout the district. On and near the
northern slopes of the Wâd et-Tibn (Wâd el-
Hummâm), from Samû'a southwards, we find many
distinct traces of vine fences, small watch-towers,
and numerous local names, which tend to show

that this region was once occupied by the cultivation of the grape, though at present no vineyards exist. In some of the yards of the Sheikhs'
houses we occasionally came across a single vine
or a few pomegranate, fig, and tobacco shrubs
planted with vegetables, as in a kitchen garden.

The climate of Northern 'Ajlûn is good, as
there are no places where stagnant waters collect
to produce miasmas, but the hot winds of the Ghôr
raise the temperature in summer to a higher degree
than is found in Jaulân, which latter country is
protected from hot winds by its vicinity to the
Lake of Tiberias. Between the latter half of May
and the middle of June, 1885, the thermometer
registered the following temperatures :—

Morning, 6 A.M., an average temperature of 19°·4 C.
(66°·5 F.).
Morning, 10 A.M., an average temperature of 30°·1 C.
(86° F.).
Evening, 6 P.M., an average temperature of 24°·8 C.
(76° F.).

Our maximum was at Et Taiyibeh, at the end
of June, when the thermometer marked 35°·5 C.
(95° F.) ; our minimum was at Semû'a on the 4th
of June, viz., 13°·75 C. (56° F.) On the 10th, 11th,
and 12th of June, we were surprised by heavy

showers of rain which lasted the whole day. As a comparison, the average temperature at Haifa, on the sea coast, may be given. On the same days the temperature registered was :—

At 6 o'clock in the morning, 17°·6 C. (63° F.).
„ 10 „ „ „ 27°·7 C. (81° F.).
„ 6 „ „ evening, 25°·6 C. (78° F.).

The maximum temperature at Haifa was found to have occurred on the 2nd June, at 11 o'clock in the morning, viz., 33° C. (91° F.), while the minimum occurred on the 23rd and 30th of May, during the night, when the thermometer registered 19° C. (66° F.).

Snow falls once in every two or three years in the Nâhiyets of Es-Siru, El-Wustîyeh, El-Kefarât, and Beni Juhma, but hardly remains more than a couple of days, but in the Kûra District and in the Jebel 'Ajlûn snow falls every year abundantly.

Population.

The nine and thirty inhabited villages comprised in the present Map, together with the Bedawîn tribes (but exclusive of Tibneh) number together a population of about 10,460 souls, or average 48 to a square mile. About the same area of country in

Haurân, as given in "Across the Jordan" (namely, 240 square miles), and containing five and twenty inhabited villages, gave a population of 10,290 souls, or about an average of 43 to a square mile. The native population of the Nâhiyets of Northern 'Ajlûn are, with minor exceptions, all Mohammedans; at Hôfa two Christian native families live very peaceably beside the general Moslem community of the town, and at Irbid we discovered among the storekeepers both Christians and Jews, besides some immigrants from Nâblus. A score of years ago the Christian population of 'Ajlûn must have numbered some hundreds, but they have all emigrated and are now settled at El-Husn, a large town, about 5 miles south of Irbid, where they form a considerable section of the population. The present inhabitants of Northern 'Ajlûn are all relations or connections of certain great Sheikh families of Kefr Yûba, Irbid, El-Bâriha, Malka, Tibneh, Kefr Esad, Beit Râs, and other large villages. These families, it is said, have lived for centuries in 'Ajlûn, and have always succeeded in maintaining their possessions against the attacks of the rapacious Bedawîn tribes. Of old, when settled in larger numbers, they successfully defended their rights against their enemies from the desert, but finally they were compelled to buy themselves off by paying the *Khuwwât* (literally, brother-right)

exacted of them, which consisted in large quantities
of grain and flocks, paid to the victorious Bedawîn
tribes. Nearly all the older Sheikhs can tell of the
hard battles they have fought, and they bear scars
of stabs with the lance, sabre-cuts, and gun-shot
wounds on their bodies. The unsafe condition
of 'Ajlûn is well described by the travellers
Burkhardt and Seetzen in the beginning of the
present century, and this insecurity continued in
'Ajlûn for a longer period than in either Jaulân
or Northern Haurân, where the Turkish Government, after repulsing the attacks of Ibrahim Pasha
(of Egypt) on Syria (1840), undertook the asser-
tion of its rights by energetic measures in the
Trans-Jordan countries. The Bedawîn tribes were
driven southwards, and were obliged to abandon
the grassy fields of Jaulân and to cross the
Yarmûk; but they settled the more securely in
the districts of 'Ajlûn, and chose the Wâd el-'Arab
especially as a lurking place for their robber forays.
The insecurity had arrived at such a pitch in
Northern 'Ajlûn that between 1840 and 1850
the peaceful inhabitants (the only payers of
Government taxes) had decided to leave the
country. The Government, however, at last decided to attack the disturbers of public peace,
and, sending out a sufficient number of cavalry
with strict orders to exterminate the clans

of highwaymen whose presence prevented the
prosperous development of 'Ajlûn, the soldiers
for once did not neglect their duty. Beginning at the Wâd el-'Arab, at this period the
camping ground of the 'Arab es-Sa'âidi, who
had violently dispossessed the proprietors of the
Wustîyeh District, they attacked them, and,
with the aid of the villagers, exterminated the
whole Bedawîn tribe down to its last member.
" The floods of the Wâd el-'Arab were tinged
with the blood of the Sa'âidi," as an eye-witness
told me, to whom I owe the above account,
"and the corpses of the slain covered its slopes.
We buried the enemy below those great isolated
rocks yonder, on the northern slopes of the Wâdy,
at the place still called *Kala' es-'Sa'âidi*, the Rocks
of the Sa'âidi tribe." In passing these rocks at a
later date, I opened with a hoe the entrances to
the caves below, which were carefully built up
with stones, and discovered within piles of human
skulls and bones with pieces of rotten clothes,
and thus verified what my informant had told me.

The villagers of Northern 'Ajlûn are now left
in peace, for the different clans of the Beni Sakher
fled southwards to Jebel 'Ajlûn and the Ghôr, and
the position of the Bedawîn who remained, as for
instance, the 'Arab Sukhûr el-'Alâ, has entirely
changed. Several elders of that tribe were pointed

out to me, who, as I was informed, forty years ago used to levy the *Khuwwât* on the village of Kefr Esad and its Sheikh, but they now herd the flocks of the very Sheikh over whom they had formerly tyrannized. General security, however, returned but slowly to the country, for its natural character renders it a fit place for the trade of the highwayman. Even to the present day the Wâd el-'Arab is notorious for its insecurity, as I myself had opportunity to remark, for the only guides we could obtain to show us the defiles were, as we afterwards learnt, highwaymen, who were engaged by our soldiers without our knowledge, the latter merely remarking to them that "if a hair of our heads was touched their hearts would be taken alive out of their bodies." I have every reason to praise their knowledge of local names, their attention to our wants, and the polite manner in which they guided us; and I cannot do better than recommend these gentlemen very strongly to all future explorers of this region.

At Hôfa I was told that the Khuwwât was levied upon the village as late as three years back by the Beni Sukhûr Arabs.

The villagers of 'Ajlûn are a kindly and hospitable people if the guest they entertain is a person properly recommended to them; otherwise much suspicion is often met with by foreigners. They are tall, sturdy men, not quite so dark skinned as are the Fellahîn of the Haurân, and less strong, and showing less self-confidence than the latter, probably also they are less brave. This latter characteristic is attributable to the fact that they are rapidly falling a prey to the usurers of Tiberias and Damascus, and are more persecuted and oppressed than their neighbours in Haurân, who are beginning to suffer from the same curse, in spite of their remote geographical position. The physical stamina of the Fellahîn of 'Ajlûn is lower on account of their poor food, the crops of 'Ajlûn being much inferior to those of the rich Haurân, and the land here is cultivated with more trouble and pains than is needed in the territories of their eastern neighbours, whose rich fields seldom lack a golden harvest.

The family life and the manners and customs of the Fellahîn of Northern 'Ajlûn are partly those found throughout Palestine proper, and partly those of the Bedawîn nomads. The ordinary villager marries but one wife, while the rich Sheikh allows himself as many as four, each wife performing (as in Jaulân) her daily duties of housekeeping for her husband, and tending the cattle and flocks according to her *dôr*, or turn of out-door service. Jealousy and quarrelsomeness often play havoc with the husband's peace ; each wife tries to limit her labours to the preparation of dainty dishes for the Sheikh, in order by this means to find favour in his eyes. Personal conflicts are not rare, and the solving of the domestic problem depends on the more or less energetic interference of the master of the house. If one of the wives becomes too quarrelsome, or seriously excites the disfavour of her husband, she is without ceremony sent back to her father and mother, and is said to be *matrûdi* (expelled). While absent on a journey to the town a good part of the Sheikh's time is generally wasted in choosing small presents for his women-kind at home, and woe to the unhappy Sheikh if all his presents are not of equal value.

Schools, with the exception of some at Irbid, are unknown in 'Ajlûn; though the Khatêb (priest) of a populous town occasionally instructs privately the sons of the Sheikh. The Mohammedan population are strict in their religious observances, and attend to the observance of the Moslem ritual as devoutly as do the Fellahîn of Haurân. I cannot say that they treated us with any great show of hostility, but as is commonly the case in these remoter countries, every new and unaccustomed sight was an object of suspicion and alarm to them. If the explorer wishes to become popular he must write as little as possible in his note-book when in their presence. He must never ask for information in regard to population or the amount of cultivated land. These people have been so ground down by their oppressors that they have not yet learned that men exist who honestly wish their welfare and do not grudge them the prosperity of their country. During centuries they have been compelled to live in constant fear for their lives and goods, and ever ready to protect themselves against the attacks of the enemy.

At Kefr Yûba, a large and populous town, I suffered from some want of courtesy from the head Sheikh, who lived in a sort of fortress, built by his predecessors, and who still preserved, surrounded by his bondsmen, the exclusiveness of a former age, and proudly rejected every friendly advance on the part of an *Abu Burneita*, "the man in a hat," as they call any European. I heard that he was wont to practise this conduct towards every unwelcome foreigner, and I respected this exclusiveness of the old 'Ajlûn noble, so seldom met with in the country nowadays, as far as I could, but when hospitality and entertainment were denied me, was obliged to protest. These are things which may in Europe be considered as matters to be freely rendered at the pleasure of the host, but among the Arabs their hospitality is subject to regular rules, the violation of which must be considered a violation of law and custom. I gave the Sheikh's

C

humour free play, and, knowing me to be a Franji, he soon began to be impolite, which he showed by withholding from me the privilege of precedence due to every *Deif*, or guest. This offence, to his great astonishment, I instantly noticed by refusing his attendance in the room, and adding that I knew that his duty required him to entertain every Government officer (such as I was) with scrupulous courtesy. I then rose and retired to my tent. On the following day one of his relations came to see me and ask pardon for the affront he had put on me. I persisted that it would be my duty to report it to the Government unless the Sheikh himself appeared and declared before a public assembly that he had been in the wrong, and asked pardon for his rudeness. This he ultimately agreed to, and carried out.

To seal this act of reconciliation he then asked us to dinner, and on the evening of the same day a great feast was prepared, sufficient to feed the entire population of the town. In groups they sat about the place, and according to their rank sat near or far from the supper trays. It is the custom on these occasions for the host, in order to disarm suspicion, to taste the meat first, and with the customary *tafaddalu*, literally, " take advantage," then to invite his guests to follow his lead. On this present occasion, as the Sheikh had violated the rights of his guest, I had to replace him, and had to take on myself the post of the *Sâhib el-Mahal,* or the proprietor of the house. I therefore began, took a piece of bread, dipped it into the dish containing cooked mutton, rice, "*freeky*" (a mass of green and dried wheat), and vegetables, and, turning to the real host, asked him repeatedly to "take advantage." After much ceremony, during which endless polite phrases were exchanged, he, the Sheikh, finally took up his bread, and with a loud *Bism Allah Rahmân er Rahîm,* "in the name of God the Merciful, the Compassionate," set the example, when hands and jaws began their duty among the rest of the assembly. After dinner we were gratified with some fine Mokha coffee which the Sheikh had himself brought home with him from the Pilgrimage to Mekka and Medina.

The night after this feast of reconciliation an assault was directed against my small camp, and the assailants demanded that we should leave forthwith. We remained armed and on the watch until the morning, when fresh cries arose demanding our instant departure. I sent for the Sheikh, and as he did not appear I gave my Firmân from the Vali (Governor-General of Syria) to one of my soldiers, and ordered him to galop to Irbid, which lay only a few miles off, and to request the

Governor of that town to send some soldiers
to protect us against the villagers. The Zaptîyeh
was hardly a few hundred yards on his journey
before the most prominent villagers ran up, and.
grasping the situation of affairs, mounted and raced
behind the soldier, begging him (*Min shân Allah*),
" for God's sake," to return, offering to deliver up
those who had been the cause of the night's dis-
turbance. Although the Zaptîyeh had little wish
to return, he finally, over-persuaded, was lifted
down from his horse and brought back to the
tent. I was then requested to break up my camp
and leave, though another meal of reconciliation
was first prepared, which, however, I could not
accept.

I was then obliged to go in to Irbid and make
my complaint against the Sheikh, who, it proved,
had been the ringleader in the late assault. In a
few hours he was brought in and made to repent
in the *habes* (prison) at Irbid, that he had thus
repeatedly violated the duties of a host, and I trust
he may have learned by this time to treat even the
much hated European traveller with proper respect.
I have since heard that, after finally obtaining
his release, the Sheikh now declares that the "old
times" are evidently past and gone, and laments
that he has been compelled in his old age "to
salute even a Franji's hat." The treatment I

received at the hands of this Sheikh is, however, an exception to the rule, and I almost invariably found the other village Sheikhs both courteous and obliging.

I was often told that if an inhabitant of 'Ajlûn swears by the *'Aûd*—any species of rod—his word can be trusted. This oath is also held sacred in Haurân and in some districts among the Bedawîn of Western Palestine. The person who is desired to swear by this oath seizes any sort of rod, or twig (often for convenience merely a straw stem is held between the fingers), and recites aloud the following words:

"*Bi hayât hal 'Aûd, wa er Rabb, el-Ma'bûd, wa Kussat Suleimân ibn Daûd, la khant, wa lâ amart min al khân.*"

بحيوة هذا العود والربّ المعبود و قسة سليمان ابن داود لا خنت و لا امرت من الخان .

Literally translated this means:

"By the life of this rod! and by the Lord, who is adored, and by the story of Solomon the son of David! verily I have not deceived nor ordered to commit any fraud."

Another class among the inhabitants of 'Ajlûn is formed by the immigrants from Jebel Nâblus (Samaria). These have settled at Mukhraba, at

Umm Keis, Deir es-Sa'neh, and some other places. They are a very conservative race, holding firmly to the customs of their country, and are less friendly and less hospitable than the native 'Ajlûnis, though evidently more industrious and more intelligent. Their dialect, as well as their clothes, betray their origin ; they wear, in addition to the long blue and white shirt of the ordinary Fellah, a pair of wide pantaloons with a short 'Abâ or mantle, and the men are remarkable for their stout figures. It is surprising how these Nâblus people have spread over the country, generally numbers of not less than ten or twelve families having settled in one spot ; I met them at Fuleh and 'Affuleh, in the Plain of Esdraelon, at Shutta, and also near Beisân, in Haurân and in 'Ajlûn, but they never seemed to be popular, but rather to be disliked by the other Fellahîn on account of their close and reserved character.

Negroes are found in small numbers and in subordinate positions among the villagers of 'Ajlûn. The small negro tribe of 'Arab el-Abîd, who graze their flocks on the northern slopes of the Wâd el-'Arab, say that the Sudân was their original home.

Near Esh Shûni some people from the Lebanon districts have settled to cultivate the Ghôr.

Such are the present inhabitants of 'Ajlûn. The

designation " *Siklâb*," given to the Wâdy in the
southern part of this Map, as well as to certain fine
springs in the lower part of the Wâd el-Hummâm,
would tend to prove that in former times a
Slavonian race was once settled in this region.

The houses of the commonalty of the 'Ajlûnis
consist of one or two small rooms, built up from
the hewn stones of ancient buildings and mortared
with white clay. The roof is formed with branches
of oak and is plastered over with *bankâda* or white
clay, which is removed every year and a new coat-
ing set in its place. A yard is added to the
dwelling as a fold for the cattle, goats, and sheep.
The houses of the sheikhs contain additional rooms
for guests, and each wife receives a room for her
private use. A large yard surrounds the whole, in
the centre of which a cistern is commonly found.
If the great room, or "menzûl," where travellers
are entertained, be too broad to be covered by
single oak branches, an arch is spanned across,
dividing the room into two equal halves; one of
which contains the "nukra," or depression in the
floor, where coffee is cooked and a fire kept up
during the winter season ; while the other portion
of the chamber is covered with mats and carpets
for the use of distinguished guests, where they
may dine and also take their night's repose.
These upper seats I generally avoided, for

they usually are populated with vermin of all
kinds. In preference I generally managed to get

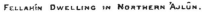

FELLAHÍN DWELLING IN NORTHERN 'AJLÛN.

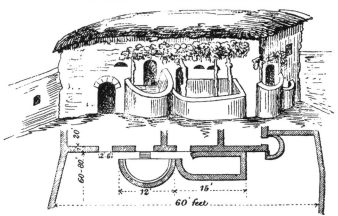

my bed spread in one of the small circular
chambers added to the main building. The floor
is here raised some 3 or 4 feet above the outer
yard, and is nicely smoothed with white clay mixed
with straw, being surrounded by a wall containing
holes for oil lamps, etc., the whole covered by a
tent roof of branches and leaves. These alcoves
have the great advantage of not being smoky,
and do exceedingly well in summer to pass a
night in. In Haurân and Jaulân similar cabins
are also found, but rather in the form of large
rectangular *Mensûls* or *Divans*, while in 'Ajlûn

they form merely additional alcoves, one being often added to the room apportioned to each wife. This she keeps well dusted, and decorates with all sorts of household ornaments, such as jars and glass bottles, coloured stones, and any prints that she may be able to acquire.

As already stated, the building material generally found in 'Ajlûn is the crumbling-limestone, very inferior in all ways to the basaltic stone of the Haurân. The style of architecture is therefore not so characteristic as that seen in Haurân. The ancient and the modern 'Ajlûnis have been forced to but little pains in the erecting of their dwellings, since Nature has provided them gratis with wood to cover the roofs and with stone to burn for lime to make mortar ; while in Haurân there are only long basalt slabs for the roof covering, and great blocks of hard building stone, which, however, when once worked, may dispense with mortar of any kind. The Haurân method of construction is, of course, the more durable, and in many instances we see buildings in Haurân dating from very ancient times intact at the present day. On the other hand, very few ancient monuments are found in Northern 'Ajlûn, on account of the crumbling building stone in use there.

The rearing of bees is one of the industries of 'Ajlûn. Bee-hives are found in nearly every village, and in the Wâd el-Arab the explorer frequently comes across the nests of the wild honey-bee.

Flocks and herds are not very numerous in 'Ajlûn, but in summer these present a better appearance than those found in Haurân, on account of the richer pasture of the southern country.

The occupation of the natives is confined to the cultivation of the soil and the breeding of cattle. Some few find work in attending to the numerous mills of the Wâd el-'Arab and Wâdy Zahar. The millers consider themselves as of a superior race to the ordinary Fellahîn. We were lucky enough to find one of these *Malem et Tawahin*, or mill-masters, ready to serve us as a guide, and as far as this part of his duties was concerned, we had nothing to complain of. But the moment we approached a mill he became so insupportably proud and overbearing in his manner towards his companions, that on one occasion he received a good thrashing at their hands as a set-off for his insolence.

ROADS.

The main line of communication in 'Ajlûn is the Darb el-Ekfûl (or Kefûl), which runs from the

Jordan Bridge, called the Jisr el-Mejâmia, across the Ghôr to Esh Shûni, and passing Ma'âd, ascends the western slopes of the Jordan cleft and then goes straight across the District of the Wustîyeh and Beni Juhma to the chief town of Irbid. After Irbid the road bifurcates, one branch running in a north-easterly direction to Er Rumta, in Haurân, and the other branch turning south-east to El-Husn, Jerash, and other towns, and finally running into the great Haj road leading to Mekka. This main road, although it is in no sort of way kept in repair, is tolerably good for horse traffic, with only moderate ascents, and is evidently the remains of an old Roman road.

A second line of communication, called the Darb as-Sultâni, passes up the slopes of the Ghôr from Tiberias to Umm Keis, the ancient city of Gadara. This road follows the watershed between the Yarmûk and the Wâd el-'Arab, and runs due east to near Ain et-Turâb, and from thence to Ed Derâ'ah and the Haurân.

Beside this road, running eastwards from Umm Keis are seen the ruins of an ancient aqueduct, the remains of which, as well as the ancient pavement of the road bordering it, prove the Roman character of its origin. This latter roadway could, with little expense, be rendered available for wheeled vehicles starting from Umm Keis. Three straight lines of

roadways, evidently dating from ancient times, run
westwards across the plain of Ard el-Alâ, down the
slopes of the Ghôr, coming together at Esh Shûni,
where they join the above-mentioned main road
crossing 'Ajlûn from west to east.   The other roads
in the country are of less importance.   One from
Umm Keis goes to Kefr Essad, and on thence to
Kumeim, Et Taiyibeh, Samû'a, and Tibneh, and
is much frequented, but is in a very bad condition, crossing up and down the steep Wâdies,
and is extremely fatiguing both for horse and
rider.

The only preference these roads have over those
of Jaulân is that the traveller may here rest at times
under the shady oaks which border the way.   The
road along the winding course of the Wâd el-'Arab
is remarkable for its picturesque scenery, the
primitive corn mills which stand beside the mur-
muring river, which is everywhere overgrown with
a jungle of cane, willow, oleander and other shrubs.
The small green valleys which run up from the
banks of the river, near where the gorge opens
into the Ghôr of the Jordan, are recommended as
fine camping grounds, if the party be sufficiently
numerous to keep in check the rapacity of the
Arabs of the Beni Sukhûr el-Ghôr.

A line of telegraph, with a service in the Arabic
language, runs down from Damascus to Irbid, and

connects this town with Sheikh Saad, the capital of Haurân.

In the following pages a detailed description is given of the villages, ancient sites, Wâdies, and other features marked on this Map. The articles are classed according to the various Nâhiyets or districts. After describing the principal village of each district, the remaining places are arranged in alphabetical order.

CHAPTER II.

THE NÂHIYET OR DISTRICT OF ES-SIRU.

THE Nâhiyet es-Siru is bounded on the north by
the Yarmûk River; on the east by the Wâdy
Samar and the Nâhiyet el-Kefarat; on the south
by the Wâd el-Arab, the Nâhiyets of El-Wustîyeh,
and Beni Juhma; and on the west by the Jordan
Ghôr. The district consists, physically, of a
mountain shoulder, furrowed with steep ravines
leading down to the rivers which bound it on all
sides. In these ravines are springs which, though
giving but a medium supply of water, are in
greater number here than in the other Nâhiyets of
the Irbid Kada.

The two chief towns of Es-Siru are Umm Keis
and Malka.

Umm Keis.—The name is pronounced by
the people Mkeis. The town lies 1,193 feet
above the Mediterranean. This is the most
important township, as well as one of the
most ancient sites on the present Map. The

Plan of
UMM KEIS
surveyed by
G. SCHUMACHER, C.E.
1886.

To el Mezra'a

To el Hammeh

To el Hammeh

To el Birket and Tiberias

Derb er Raseifeh

Paved road

Ruins of Villas and Villas

El Burj
(castle)

To the Jisr el Mejamia

Derb el 'Ajlony

Wâdi el Arab

Wâdi el Arab

Wâdi el Arab

El Melab

West Theatre

West Thermae

Tower

Caves

Caves

Caves

Ruins of Dora

Ruins

Vault

North Theatre

North Mausoleum

Ancient Mausoleum

Sarcophagi

'Ayûn es Senniyeh

Tomb

Village

Wâdi el Budneh

Kûm el Keis

Umm Keis

Caves

Caves

Road to Haurân

Aqueduct

To 'Ain Umm Keis and Haurân

Scale of Feet.
0   100 200 300 400 500 600 700 800 900 1000

F.S. Weller, lith.

town is situated at the extreme north-western
border of the high land of Northern 'Ajlûn, and
commands a magnificent view over the Lake of
Tiberias, Southern Jaulân, the Yarmûk Valley
(with the hot baths in the gorge below), the Ghôr
and Jordan, Galilee, and Mount Tabor. There
could hardly be found a second point in this part
of 'Ajlûn which combines so perfectly the advantages due to a magnificent soil and a commanding
position. Towards the north, steep slopes border
the site of the town, which spread out below
into a wide plain ending at the hot baths on the
Yarmûk. Westwards extends the rich plain of
Ard el - Alâ, covered with rich cornfields. A
narrow shoulder runs for many miles eastwards,
forming a natural roadway connecting this district
with lands of the Haurân ; while southwards the
wooded slopes descend right down to the Wâd el-
'Arab. Umm Keis is thus naturally protected to
the north and south, and partly also to the westward, for the Wâd el-Fakhed comes up to and
surrounds the town as far as El-Kasr, leaving but
a narrow neck between this and the Khallet ed-
Dôra. On the east side a strong wall has been
erected to guard the approach to the town.

Umm Keís, by competent authorities, is considered to represent the Roman Gadara. Here the
pleasure-loving Romans, after having enjoyed the

restorative effects of the hot springs of Amatha (El-Hammi), retired for refreshment, enjoying the cooler heights of the city, and solacing their leisure with the plays performed in the theatre. Gadara was the metropolis of Peræa, and a city of the Decapolis. Josephus ("Wars," iv, 7, § 3) speaks of it as "a place of strength, containing many rich citizens," and describes in detail its capture by Vespasian, from the hands of the insurgent Jews. In his "Wars" (iii, 7, § 1) the same author states that "villas and small cities lay round about Gadara." In the preceding age Alexander Jannæus had conquered the city after a siege of ten months. Pompey had rebuilt Gadara, because his freedman, Demetrius, was born there. The Jews held a Sanhedrim in this city and Augustus gave Gadara to Herod the Great, but re-annexed it to Syria after the death of that ruler. The city contained for the most part pagan inhabitants; but in later times became the residence of one of the bishops of Palestina Secunda. In regard to its original name, *Gadara*, Herr Socin* states that it is still preserved in the name of the caves of "Jedâr" near the town. This statement I can confirm, seeing that the eastern part of the site of the town, near El-Butmi, is undermined with a

---

* Bädecker's "Palestine," English edition, p. 398.

great number of caves, and is known to the natives as " Jedûr Umm Keis."

Coming from the north and riding up the plain from El-Hammi, we reached a steep ascent, where the rider is obliged to pick his way among heaps of *débris* consisting of great building stones and fragments of column capitals and shafts, which have rolled down from the ruins above. Following the steep road along the Wâd el-Bareighît we

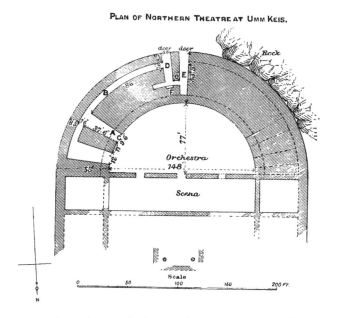

PLAN OF NORTHERN THEATRE AT UMM KEIS.

enter the ruins and the modern town near a large terebinth called El-Butmi or Butmi Umm Keis.

D

On this part of the ancient site, miserable huts have been erected by the settlers, while others have built themselves abodes in the numerous caves in the Wâdy bank. The entire population may number about 200 souls ; they cultivate tobacco round their huts, vegetables on the adjacent slopes, and grain on the corn lands of the Ard el-'Alâ. They are, however, a lazy and boorish set, showing especial unfriendliness towards foreigners, as do all the immigrants from Nâblus. They draw their water supply from 'Ain Umm Keis, a spring in the wâdy, to the south.

Lying close to the modern village, and to the west, is the narrow mountain shoulder, the summit of which forms an elevated plateau. Here is seen the ancient site of Gadara, called El-Mel'ab by the natives. This word, which may be rendered the "place of play," is probably derived from the theatre which stands on the border of the plateau to the north. This was the Northern Theatre. From it you overlook the Jaulân and the Yarmûk Valley, the hot baths of Amatha, and part of the Lake of Tiberias. In diameter the orchestra measures 148 feet, its radius being 77 feet ; the exterior total diameter of the theatre gave 254 feet. The building is in a very much ruined condition, and most of the building stones have been shaken horizontally and moved from their places,

probably by earthquakes. The number of the rows
of benches, running in semicircular lines, can no

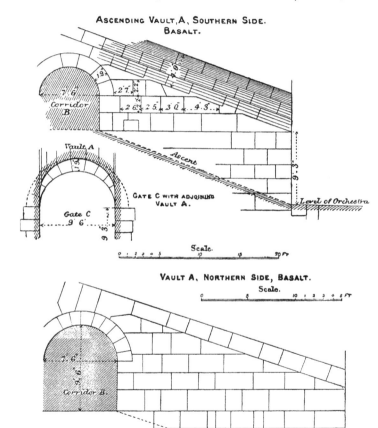

ASCENDING VAULT, A, SOUTHERN SIDE.
BASALT.

VAULT A, NORTHERN SIDE, BASALT.

longer be counted, and the interior disposition
of the stage can only partly be made out. The

western part of the theatre is cut out in the live
rock. To the north of the orchestra a proscenium
was built, but its dimensions remain doubtful.
Traces of a sort of gateway, or main entrance,
flanked with columns, can yet be seen lying north
of the stage. The benches rise one above the
other in a semicircle, and are supported on long

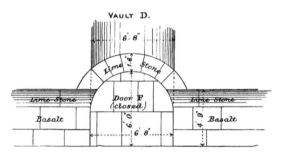

VAULT D.

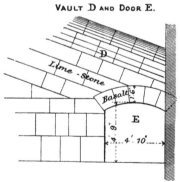

VAULT D AND DOOR E.

vaulted passage ways ; these vaults are extremely
well built, for the most part of basalt blocks, care-

fully hewn, and joined without mortar. The joints are now broken and are from one-sixth to one-quarter of an inch wide, some being less. The method of building will be seen in the annexed sketch. The vault, A, leads up from the orchestra to the vaulted corridor, B, and back to the outer wall of the theatre (see p. 49, Plan).

The vaulted gateway, D, is partly built of basalt, and partly of soft limestone blocks ; the latter having been cut with a broad edged chisel, the marks of which may yet be seen. The annexed sketch shows the vault, D, with a door, F, which evidently has been built up at a later epoch.

The benches of the amphitheatre are of basalt. The seats had a width of $28\frac{1}{4}$ inches, with a height of $17\frac{1}{2}$ inches. The subjoined sketch shows the section of the carving :—

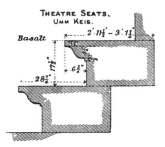

THEATRE SEATS,
UMM KEIS.

The city wall, which surrounds the elevated plateau called El-Mel'ab, encloses the theatre on its northern side, the theatre wall thus forming a part of the city fortifications. Close to where the proscenium ends we found traces of a large eastern gate, measuring 16 feet 8 inches wide flanked with pillars, and a paved road running

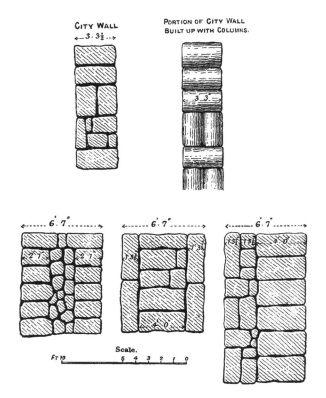

thence through the city nearly due west. The city wall varies in its thickness, in some parts it is only 3 feet 3½ inches across, in others 6 feet 7 inches, this last measurement being on the south, where the slopes are easily accessible, and here two strong towers were erected. The wall is now almost a complete ruin, but the remains show that the masonry was good, being generally of limestones, with a few basalt blocks, fitted without mortar.

A few hundred yards to the west of the Northern Theatre just described, but still within the city wall, is found the Western Theatre, which is in a less ruined state than is the northern edifice. The Western Theatre

WESTERN THEATRE, UMM KEIS.

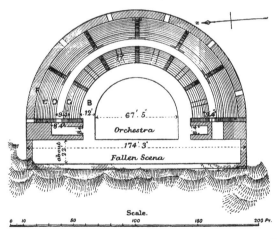

is entirely built with well-hewn basalt blocks

The orchestra measures 67 feet 5 inches in
diameter, and the main front of the theatre is
174 feet 3 inches across.   The seats are built in
a semicircle, with fifteen rows, and stairways
in between. A fine circular vault, with doors
opening towards the interior and the exterior of
the theatre, runs in a semicircle, below the seats,
and must have served as a convenient approach
to them.   The centre stairway is distinguished by
having at its upper extremity an ornamented
tribune. The orchestra is somewhat sunk below
the level ; immediately above it is a semicircular
platform (B), 12 feet wide, from which the stairways begin to ascend.   Three feet above this bench
commence the lowest of the first five seat-rows (C) ;
then there is a gangway, 9 feet 4 inches wide (D),

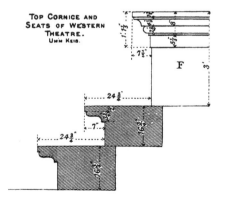

TOP CORNICE AND
SEATS OF WESTERN
THEATRE.
Umm Keis.

on to which the doors of the semicircular vault

above described open in the perpendicular wall, 6 feet 10 inches high, which backs the gangway. Above this are ten seat-rows (E), enclosed by a wall (F), 3 feet high, with a fine cornice running along the top, and with this wall, which attains a height of 35 feet from the ground, the building apparently ceased, though possibly two or three more rows of seats may still have been added above.

The theatre stands free on a sloping piece of ground, and commands a magnificent view over the Ghôr, Northern 'Ajlûn, Tabor, and the Lake of Tiberias. The remains are well preserved, but

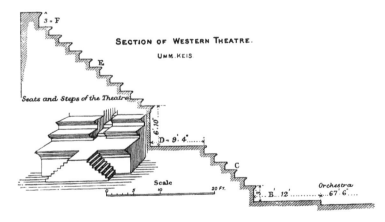

SECTION OF WESTERN THEATRE.

UMM.KEIS

Seats and Steps of the Theatre

Scale

the stones have been horizontally displaced, show-ing that earthquakes have co-operated in the work of ruin. The remains would lead us to con-

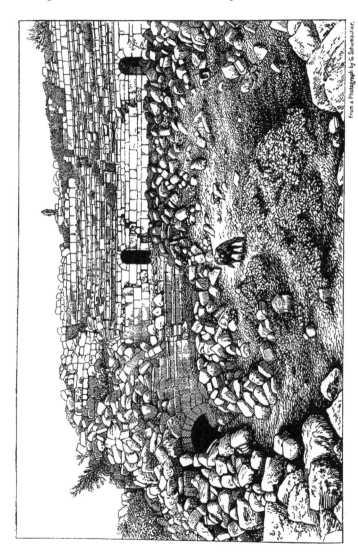

From a Photograph by G. Schumacher.

WESTERN THEATRE UMM KEIS, VIEW FROM THE WEST.

From a Photograph by G Schumacher.

WESTERN THEATRE UMM KEIS, CIRCULAR VAULT BELOW THE SEATS.

clude that a proscenium existed formerly on the
west side, and this must have been about 22 feet
in width.

Immediately to the north of this theatre I
discovered traces of a basilica or church, built with
three naves, the interior length of which measured
74 feet 7 inches. The width of the main nave,
which had an apse on the northern end, was
24 feet 10 inches, that of each of the side naves

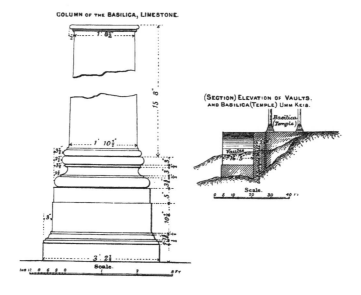

COLUMN of the BASILICA, LIMESTONE.

(SECTION) ELEVATION OF VAULTS.
AND BASILICA (TEMPLE) UMM KEIS.

being 14 feet inside. The side walls of this
basilica were composed of rows of columns, the
northern and southern walls alone being solid, as is

shown in the annexed plan. This church is a ruin
to its very foundations, and the beautiful columns
are rapidly breaking up ; a sufficient number, however, were still *in situ* to enable the building to

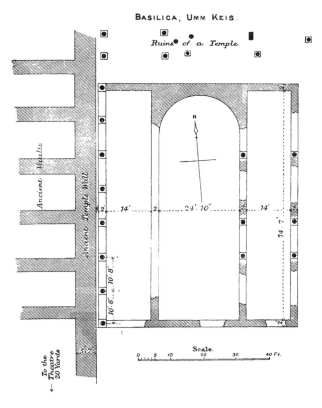

BASILICA, UMM KEIS.

be planned. The length of the columns was
15 feet 6 inches in most specimens ; the upper

diameter of the shaft was 2 feet, the lower 2 feet 2 inches; some, however, measured 1 foot 8¼ inches above, and 1 foot 10½ inches below. The style of architecture is that generally found in the early Christian basilicas, built under Roman influence. The capitals are Corinthian, showing an acanthus leaf border, the bases being Attic and Ionic. Fragments of the architraves lie scattered about. The material used for the stones and columns is the usual crumbling-limestone of the country.

The western side of the basilica is built close up against an ancient basalt wall, 5 feet 7 inches thick, which runs southward to the outer wall of the theatre, and northwards almost as far as the city gate. Its length is 350 feet; and in it are fourteen vaults, apparently used as ovens, which were added at a later date. To the north of the basilica is a level tract of land which extends as far as the gate and the main road. Scattered over this ground are numerous column-shafts, capitals, bases, architraves, blocks of well-hewn building stones, and other fragments of building materials, generally of the crumbling-limestone. Some of the bases were found to be still standing *in situ*, but their number was not sufficient to enable the plan of the building they supported to be drawn up. All that can be stated is, that this ancient basalt wall and the scattered columns must have originally belonged

to a temple, which of old stood on the site
which the basilica afterwards occupied ; and that
the western colonnade of this ancient temple was
probably incorporated into the basilica. The lower
part of the temple wall was supported on vaults
constructed of basalt blocks well-hewn, and
showing a curious joint, as may be seen in the
annexed drawing.

HOLES IN THE WALLS OF THE VAULTS.

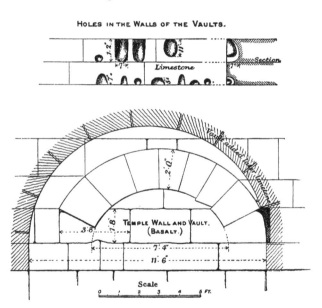

In the walls of the vaults, and probably dating
from a later date than the original building of the
temple, holes are seen of various sizes and shapes,

which evidently were used for holding oil lamps. Their openings bear no sign of ever having been closed by any species of door.

Leaving the temple ruin and going northwards, we reach the western city gate, which is flanked by pillars of basalt ; the cornice of the gateway is well preserved, and shows a high order of architectural design. The paved street is here of a width of 16 feet 8 inches ; two steps, the first of which was 7 feet 8 inches wide and 1 foot 4 inches high, and the second 4 feet wide and 1 foot 6 inches high, led up to the gateway, which measures 42 feet from pillar to pillar. The buildings of the gateway are too much in ruin to be distinctly traced at the present day.

The road which leads across this part of the city is flanked by a wall, and has a length of 960 feet, with a width of 16 feet 8 inches. The pavement consists of basalt blocks, roughly hewn, varying in size, and measuring from 18 to 26 inches square ; the rows run diagonally and also at right angles to the main axis of the street. The middle part is paved by a double row set parallel with the axis, and the wheel marks of the Roman vehicles can yet be traced on the stones. The width of their carriages must have been about 3 feet 1 inch from axle to axle. At a later period the width of the road was reduced to 14 feet 8 inches, and it may be noted that the level of the roadway slightly slopes towards two sides.

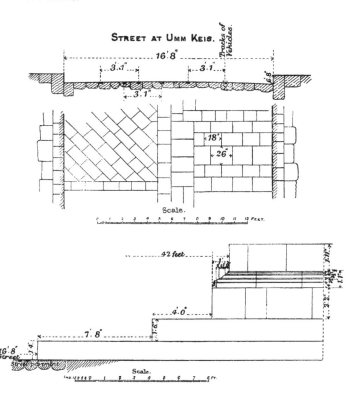

STREET AT UMM KEIS.

Scale.

In some parts the edging stones bordering the street are formed of column shafts.

On the south side of the Western Theatre we found the remains of what appeared to have been a mausoleum. This was a rectangular, almost

E

subterranean building, about 50 feet long from west to east, and measuring 21 feet across from south

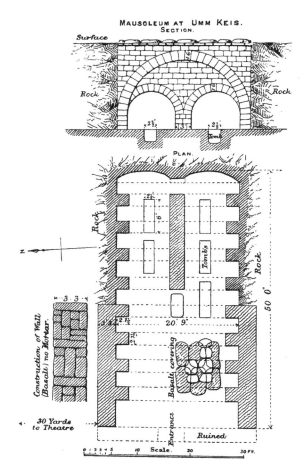

MAUSOLEUM AT UMM KEIS.

to north. The western entrance is ruined, but the

remainder of the building tolerably well preserved. Large arches span across from side to side of the western half, and the eastern half is divided into two small vaults, containing six tombs, cut deep in the flooring. Across these arches, to form the roof, basalt slabs are laid, as is usual in the Haurân buildings, and the whole space is thus covered by slabs, in place of a vaulted roof. The southern and northern parts of the building are cut out of the limestone rock on which the building stands. The construction of the basalt walls is similar to that found in Haurân ; their thickness is 3 feet 3 inches.

To judge by the style of the roof and the semi-subterranean character of this building, I presume it to be the most ancient of the monuments found at Umm Keis.

The highest point of the plateau of El Mel'ab was fortified by a strongly-built wall or some sort of rampart ; but the remains are not sufficiently well preserved to enable us to make out its original form. Outside the city wall, and little to the north-east of the northern theatre, a large number of sarcophagi are seen lying above the ground. They lie about in no sort of order, and some are also found in the houses of the present village. They are cut out of the hard basalt rock, and have, as a rule, an exterior length of 7 feet, a width of

E 2

2 feet 5 inches, and a height of 2 feet 3 inches.

SARCOPHAGUS, UMM KEIS

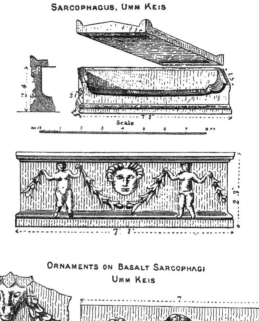

ORNAMENTS ON BASALT SARCOPHAGI
UMM KEIS

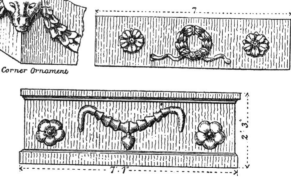

Corner Ornament

Their longer sides are ornamented with allegorical

figures and a leaf-ornament, showing rosettes, &c., and are very artistically carved. Each sarcophagus was originally covered with a stone lid, with raised edges (as shown in the accompanying sketch), which was worked to fit the frame of the upper part of the stone box.

Near the eastern city gate are the ruins of a square building, in the centre of which are a number of sarcophagi, still apparently occupying their original position; this may have been another mausoleum. These sarcophagi and those in places adjoining are oriented with the longer axis running from south-east to north-west; the stone cushion in the interior, for the support of the head, being placed on the west side, so that the face must have been turned to the rising sun.

Below the ground occupied by the present village of Umm Keis many caves, and ancient burial places, were discovered. The annexed plan will show their general disposition, and illustrate the following description.

These caves are called *Halas* by the natives. A stairway on the south side generally leads to a wide room, in the walls of which loculi are cut out. Here numerous sarcophagi were found scattered about, which are now used for bread ovens, and as receptacles for storing grain, or as mangers for the cattle. Low openings lead from the outer chamber into adjoining caverns, containing separate apartments for the sepulture of the dead. The height

CAVES OF UMM KEIS.

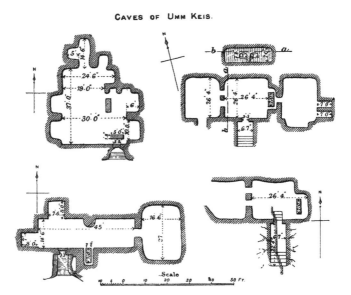

.Scale

of these caves varies from 5 to 7 feet; they are worked out of the limestone rock, and are of rectangular shape. The heaps of straw with which they were encumbered prevented our exploration of some, while others are occupied by the natives as dwelling places. I was told (and, to a certain extent, was able to verify the information) that upwards of 360 caves of the description here given exist under this ancient site, and over in the Wâd el-'Ain, and on the adjacent mountain slopes. The entrances are, as a rule, surmounted by a large basalt lintel, from one of which I copied the following inscription :—

The entrances were originally closed by stone gates, some of which still exist *in situ*, and perform their office. These gates of basalt have a really grand appearance, they are carefully carved and ornamented, and along the upper edge is carved a

ENTRANCE TO A SEPULCHRAL CAVE, UMM KEIS

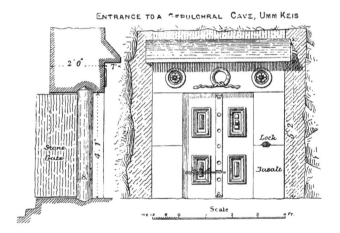

sort of cornice, which runs in a pointed angular pattern. To the right of the entrance is a species of lock, with a bolt which can be pushed home, and again withdrawn from the outside.

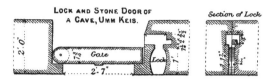

From the doorway two or three steps generally lead down to the sepulchral chamber.

On an ancient column-shaft near the entrance of one of the caves I found the following much defaced inscription :—

On the building stones of the Western Theatre and other monuments, the following collection of mason-marks were gathered. They were generally about 3½ inches long; and among them figured many crosses.

On other Monuments :

Leaving the city and going westwards, a paved road, the Derb er-Raseifîyeh, bordered by a row of column shafts on either side, crosses the narrow neck, separating Wâd el-Fakhed from the Khallet ed-Dôra, and ends at Abu en-Namel, the shrine of a Mohammedan saint, whose tomb is built up with pieces of ancient masonry. Large terebinths shade this spot, which was probably a cemetery in former times. The ground lying to the south and west of the shrine is thickly covered with ancient remnants of well-hewn building stones, and numerous fragments of basalt and limestone columns, with traces of buildings seen scattered here and there. This part of the site of Gadara may represent the locality of the " villas and small cities " of which Josephus speaks. One large building, called El-Kasr, occupying an elevated position among the other ruins, may be the remains of a castle, to judge at least from the solidity of its construction and its great size. The ruins, which extend westward from the tomb of Abu en - Namel, together with those included among the buildings of the modern town, and of the tract called Jedûr Umm Keis, cover an area which measures about one mile in the length from east to west, and has an average width of a quarter of a mile across from north to south, this area may therefore be computed at about 160 acres.

From near Abu en-Namel the paved road, called Raseifîyeh, bifurcates towards the west. At this point occur the traces of a great number of square chambers (R), standing one beside the other, each measuring in the interior dimensions 16 feet 5 inches by 21 feet 5 inches, with walls of 5 feet 6 inches, and a space of 3 feet 8 inches between each. The total length (from east to west) of this row of chambers is 698 feet ; at their western end rises a square building, with columns, flanked to the north and south by wings, with an apse in each on the west, built above a basement story of basalt stones. The general arrangement will be best understood from the annexed plan.

PLAN OF EL BIRKET, UMM KEIS.

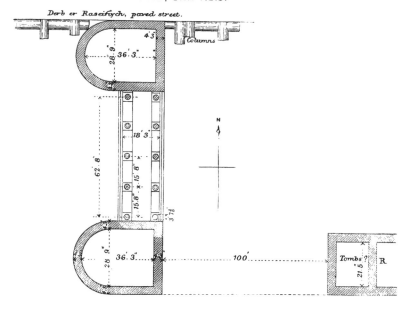

Derb er Raseifiych, paved street.

The ornamentation of the columns, whose bases still stand *in situ* on the basement, would tend to prove them of the same period as those in the Church near the Western Theatre, described on a preceding page.

These columns, which are hewn of the crumb-

ling-limestone from the vicinity, have a lower
diameter of 3 feet 7⅜ inches, their bases being
Attic. The column shaft has a length of from
5 to 6 feet, and shows at top and bottom a square
hole, 4 inches by 3 inches across, as also do those
of the basilica before described.

This building, which is named El-Birket (the
Tank) by the natives, is probably of Christian
origin, the rows of chambers adjoining having

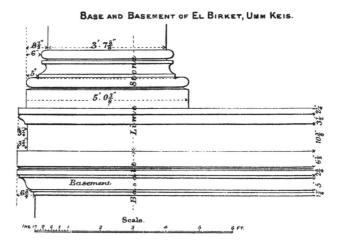

BASE AND BASEMENT OF EL BIRKET, UMM KEIS.

served either for domestic purposes (as baking
ovens) or else as tombs ; the latter supposition
would seem the more probable, and attached to the
mausoleum would have been the temple, the place
named El-Birket. This hypothesis is confirmed

by the fact that in the immediate neighbourhood,
and lying to the north-west, on the borders of the
Wâd Mâkûk, are found several tombs and caves
excavated in the soft limestone rock, and traces
of similar tombs are found close to the " Birket."
The interior of these tombs is entirely fallen in,
and they could not without some excavating be
now explored, but many sarcophagi lie about in
the neighbourhood.

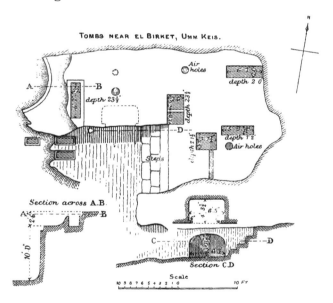

On the further side of Wâd Mâkûk is a ruin
measuring 33 feet square, built on a commanding
position ; it is the most western of the remains

at Umm Keis. Great basalt stones lie about in heaps, with a great amount of unhewn building material. It must originally have been built in the Haurân style of architecture, and is evidently extremely ancient.

In the eastern quarter of the ruins of Umm Keis runs the ancient Roman aqueduct called Kanât Fir'ûn (Pharaoh's Watercourse). It follows for some distance the road to 'Ain et-Turâb, and if the statement of the natives be correct traces of it are to be seen as far east as Ed Dera'ah, and from there northward to Dilli and Es Sunamein, in Northern Haurân. Along the Roman road from 'Ain et-Turâb to El-Kabu, the aqueduct occupies but a single channel, but after this point the channel is double, each section measuring 2 feet 8 inches in width and a foot in depth, with a stone plate, 2 feet broad, set in between. The annexed section and plan shows the portion excavated by me near Umm Keis. The side stones, measuring 2 feet cube, are replaced further to the east by smaller sized blocks. The plastering is set over a concrete of small stones, well mortared; over this come three to four layers of mortar, mixed with ashes and small pieces of stone, each layer being half an inch in thickness, and the total plastering has therefore a thickness of 5 inches. The inner surface of the channel is of a bright, glossy, yellowish colour, and is as hard as stone. There is no sign that the aqueduct was ever covered over.

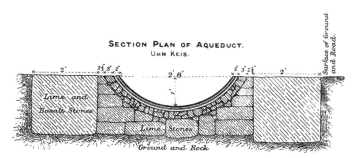

SECTION PLAN OF AQUEDUCT.
UMM KEIS.

The foregoing is a brief account of the more interesting of the remains at Umm Keis, and illustrates the character of the different buildings found on this site. With the exception of the pillar cornices and those seen at El-Birket, the style of architecture found is not remarkable, the calcareous rock used, as before noticed, not being fitted for architectural ornamentation. The quarry of basalt used was evidently the one we found on the western slopes below Umm Keis, between Khirbet el-Mikyal and Khirbet et-Tabak, where unfinished stones were seen in considerable numbers. The ornamentations cut in this hard rock are far superior in style to the limestone carvings, and no slight skill was shown in the art of cutting and hollowing out the basalt sarcophagi.

A more thorough exploration of the remains west of El-Burj, on the plain called the Ard el-'Alâ, will, it is hoped, be ultimately effected. Doubtless these hillocks cover the remains of ruined villas, and the buildings would repay a careful examination, but the plough of the fellah has already gone over a good part of these remains, and much excavation would be required.

Malka.—This spot is one of the largest and most populous villages on the present Map. The 124 stone huts composing it are, as a rule, carefully built ; they are kept well white-washed, and the place resembles in this the Druze villages of Mount Carmel. Malka contains a population of 600 Mohammedans. The streets are broad and clean, and as straight as can be expected with the fellahîn for builders. The western part of the village is surrounded by cactus hedges, and gardens (Krûm) containing fig trees and olives and vegetables. The southern extremity of the village is decorated by a neatly-kept, whitewashed, and cupolaed shrine called the Makâm esh Sheikh 'Omar.

The houses of Malka are built immediately above a precipice, on a narrow mountain ridge, of the breadth of the town, which to the east falls off abruptly into the rocky Wâd 'Ain el-Kîleh, and to the west into the Wâd 'Ain Khalîfeh. On the north is the large Wâd el-Humra. The village is thus, by nature, very well protected. Its water supply is from the 'Ain Khalîfeh, a perennial spring in the wâdy so named ; and other small springs are found in the Wâd 'Ain el-Kîleh.

The inhabitants of Malka are a pleasant people, and the Mukhtar (or village head-man) is a learned man. The excellent soil of the Sâhel ej-Juwâni grows olive trees, as also a part of the Yarmûk Valley, belonging to the villagers, near the junction of Wâd 'Ain Ghazâl and the Yarmûk River. Some of the villagers have gone into partnership with Jew merchants from Western Palestine, and have opened small dry-goods stores.

In the village itself no ancient remains were discovered, but to the west and south-west lies what would appear to be an ancient site. It covers an area measuring 450 yards in length, and the like in width, and spreads over the plateau, which is now overgrown with ancient olive trees. This site bears the name of Khirbet Malka. Nothing, however, was to be found but a few sarcophagi cut in the limestone rock, and vast heaps of *débris* containing quantities of painted potsherds. Great piles of well-hewn building stones occupy a slight elevation, and in the southern part of the plateau two buildings of a more modern appearance are still partly standing. The buildings are square in plan,

F

with a courtyard to the north. Spanned across in
the width of 18 feet 9 inches is a vaulted ceiling,

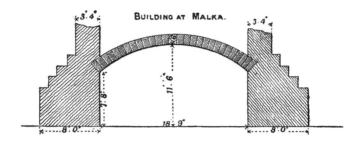

BUILDING AT MALKA.

CONSTRUCTION OF WALL.

and the lateral walls are, in their upper part, 3 feet
4 inches thick, and at the base being upwards of
8 feet. The material is hewn limestone, the blocks
being laid in mortar horizontally and diagonally;
in places also old basalt stones and ornaments
have been built up into the walls. The construction
of the vaulting is similar to that seen in the old
Haurânian mosques. I have no doubt that they
are the ruins of Mohammedan shrines, as their
present name indicates, for they are called El-
Jawâm'a, or, The Mosques.

CHAPTER III.

OTHER PLACES IN THE DISTRICT OF ES-SIRU.

'Âbis.—A small ruin on the shoulder above 'Ain es-Sahn, also called 'Ain et-Tâssi. The ruin is of little importance. The spring below is perennial, and rises in the small cave of a limestone rock in the Wâdy 'Ain es-Sahn, and flows westwards, watering a few tobacco and vegetable grounds; the water is clear as crystal and of good quality. The Wâdy has an abundant growth of Oleanders, Mallûl (Oak), Kharrub (Locust Tree), Butm (Terebinth), and 'Abhar Oak. Two hundred yards to the south the perennial spring of 'Ain Kelâb wells out from beneath a rock and joins the waters of the 'Ain es-Sahn, the two forming a charming brook, taking its course through an abundant growth of brushwood and shrubs.

'Ain el-Kusab and *'Ain Ra'ân.*—Two springs of moderate supply, flowing out on the northern slopes of Wâd el-Barûka, a gorge overgrown with cane jungle.

F 2

'Ain Umm ej-Jrein.—A small perennial spring ; above it, to the east, is the 'Ain Barûka of the same character.

'Ain et-Turâb.—A spring at the head of Wâdy Samar ; this gorge has as yet not been thoroughly explored.   There are some ruins in the neighbourhood.

'Ain es-Sukkar.—A fine spring near Malka, at the head of the Wâd el-Mallâki.

'Ain 'Atîyeh.—A small spring at the head of the Wâdy of the same name.

'Ain Fu'ara.—A spring with a good supply of water ; it is built round with ancient masonry, and has sweet, clear water.   A little above, on the northern slopes of the Wâd Fu'ara is another spring, overshadowed by a couple of wild fig trees.

'Ain Umm el-Kharâk.— A poor supply of water, and generally dry in summer.

'Ain Haîyeh.—A small spring near Tell Zara'a in the Wâd el-'Arab.

'Ain es-Smeirât.—Of a medium supply, flowing into the Wâd el-'Arab.

'Ain Umm Keis.—This spring rises in a cavern, 4 feet in width and 5 to 6 feet in the height, opening below a gigantic limestone rock ; traces of ancient masonry are seen round it.   The spring has a good supply of water of excellent flavour, and the brook from it flows into the Wâd el-'Ain,

the gorge being overgrown with a thick growth of oleanders and wild fig trees. In the vicinity is an ancient olive grove. This spring supplies the present town of Umm Keis with drinking water ; its situation in a deep valley below the ancient Gadara, rendered it impracticable to bring its waters into the ancient city, and an aqueduct was, therefore, built, bringing in the water supply from the distant hills (*see* above, page 78).

'Ain el-'Asal.—A copious spring, built round with traces of ancient masonry, lying below the ancient site of El-Kabu.

'Ain Kasaksôbeh.— A spring with its outflow overgrown with wild fig trees, situated beyond El Hammi.

'Ain Wonsa.—A spring of the same character as the above.

'Ain el-Butmi.—A spring with a permanent and plentiful supply of water, surrounded with ruined masonry, among which is found an abundant growth of Butm (terebinth) and raspberry bushes. Its waters flow through the village of El Mukhaibi, and water the vegetable gardens of the Nâblus settlers.

'Arab Sukhûr el-Ghôr. — A large tribe of Bedawîn, counting about 200 tents, who occupy the northern part of the Jordan Valley. They are a branch of the 'Arab es-Sakhr, the terror of the

Lower Ghôr; although still of truculent character, they have of late abandoned their trade of highwaymen and are now peacefully settled in the splendid tract of the Upper Ghôr. Their Sheikh, Kuweitîn Agha, is a man of proud bearing, but very hospitable towards Europeans. His father, Akîleh Agha, was at one time the Sheikh of Galilee, and twenty-five years ago disposed, at his will, of the life and property of his clansmen, who possessed all the country from Acre to Tiberias. With the 300 to 500 mounted men of his tribe he resisted for a long time all attempts on the part of the Government to subdue him. He was decorated by several European monarchs, and the crosses given him are still worn by his son. He was finally caught by a ruse and punished. A reflected splendour of the wealth of passed days is still visible in the large tent possessed by Kuweitîn Agha, but he is now in the power of a Syrian money-lender, to whom he is practically a bondsman. The main camping place of the tribe is near Ed Delhamîyeh, on the Jordan, and the village is the property of their Sheikh. The number of the clansmen is about 900 souls.

'Arab el-'Abîd.—A small and miserable tribe of negroes who occupy a part of the northern slopes of Wâd el-'Arab below Umm Keis. It is said that they have migrated hither from the Soudân,

but I was unable to learn when and why the
change was effected ; they live in about 40 tents
and number less than 150 souls.

'Arab el-Mukhaibeh.—A small Bedawîn tribe,
whose flocks graze along the borders of the
Yarmûk River, between El-Hammi and El-
Mukhaibi. During the summer season, when
hundreds of tents are set up round these hot
baths by natives from all parts of Syria, the tribe
furnishes sheep, goats, milk, butter, and vegetables
to the visitors, and thus make a small income.
Their lands—some 50 feddâns in extent—are now
no more their own, for being of excellent quality,
they have passed into the possession of the Acre
merchants, including the fertile plain round El-
Hammi, and to these merchants the tribe is now
indebted to the extent of 27,000 piastres. They
occupy some 30 tents and number 150 souls.

'Arkûb Umm Keis.—The terraced slopes bordering the main road from the Ard el-'Alâ towards
Tiberias, below Umm Keis.

'Arûk ej-Jenânîyeh.—A mountain shoulder lying
east of Umm Keis.

*'Arkûb Rûmi, 'Arkûb Umm Tûd, 'Arkûb
el-Fakîri, 'Arkûb ej-Jûk,* and *'Arkûb ed-Dweirîkh,*
five nearly parallel mountain ridges, divided by
deep ravines, extending from the northern watershed of Wâd el-'Arab northward towards the

Yarmûᴋ and the Wâdy Samar or Wâd el-Humra. Each has an average length of about two miles and a width at the upper shoulder of a few hundred yards. Some of the ridges bear traces of ruins on their northern extremities, and usually a landslip has occurred along their lateral slopes of the soft crumbling-limestone formation found here, and this has often buried the springs in the ravines. The crests of the ridges are covered by the oak forest.

'Ard el-Burz.—A tract of land bearing traces of ruins, near the ancient site of El-Burz.

'Ard el-'Alâ.—The rich plateau, with a lava soil, lying to the west of Umm Keis.

Abu en-Namel.—1. The ruin of a Mohammedan tomb, built up of the ancient remains from part of Umm Keis. A beautiful terebinth (Butm) grove surrounds it. 2. A tract of land on the southern bank of the Wâdy el-'Arab.

Birket el-'Arâis.—A natural pool of water, 130 yards square, and of rectangular shape, its shores being marshy and overgrown with rushes. The temperature of its waters on the 26th of May, 1885, was 27°·5 C. (F. 81°), that of the air at the same time being 22°·5 C. (F. 72). The waters have a slightly brackish taste, but are clear. Tortoises, frogs, and wild duck are found in or on its waters. The Birket is situated in a depression a little above the

Yarmûk, and 330 feet above Hammi. To the east, west, and the south, it is surrounded by hills, leaving an opening to the north. I presume this lakelet is formed by a hot spring, the temperature of which has cooled. There are many other such springs in the Wâd el-'Arab, and this supposition is confirmed by the observations of my travelling companion, Dr. Noetling, who discovered, in the so-called Et-Tawâka, a rocky precipice honey-combed with natural and artificial caves, bordering the western brink of the Birket, the same mineral deposits of thermal springs as are found round El-Hammi and at other places along the course of the Yarmûk.

The Birket grows larger in winter, but seemed to me ill-fitted to serve as a bathing place, though its name, "The Pool of the Brides," would seem to point to its having been used for this purpose some time in the long past.

Bayâdet 'Ulûka.—A white limestone precipice on the western slopes below Umm Keis.

Derb er Raseifîyeh.—An ancient paved road running from Umm Keis towards Tiberias (*see* above, page 73).

Derb el-'Alâ. — An ancient road still used running between Umm Keis and the Jisr el-Mejâmia.

Derb el-'Ajami.—Another ancient road leading

in a more southern direction to the same Jisr (bridge).

Derb el-Mikyal.—A branch road of Derb el-'Ala.

Dhahr el-Ahmâr.—One of the long hill crests so characteristic of the vicinity of Malka, ending in a steep precipice. Its name is owing to its curved profile, and signifies " the ass's back."

Dôkara.—A tolerably well-built village containing fifty huts and nearly 400 inhabitants ; fig and olive trees, pomegranates, and some vines, are grown here. The soil is good and fruitful ; the inhabitants are friendly and industrious. Some ancient remains and mounds of old building stones were found in the vicinity.

El-Mukhaibi.—A ruin of small extent at the junction of the Wâd 'Ain Ghazâl and the Yarmûk, built at the edge of a basaltic precipice, and occupying a commanding position overlooking part of the Yarmûk Valley. It must have been of some importance in former times, for the entire neighbourhood, down as far as the river bank, is also called El-Mukhaibi, as also the palm jungle round the hot springs, and the Bedawîn who camp there have adopted the name for their tribe. The word signifies a "hiding place," which, in fact, is the character of the spot, especially of the palm jungle round the hot baths to the east. The trees number some hundreds, and harbour wild boar and other game in abundance. I penetrated with some trouble into the jungle, but could discover no ancient remains. The hot baths of El-Hammi also belong to El-Mukhaibi. The Bedawîn have erected in the vicinity of 'Ain el-Butmi several miserable huts, which they use as grain stores and as refuges in winter. A little below the ruins, at the eastern end of the jungle, is a primitive flour mill, worked by the outflow of a hot spring called the Hammet esh Sheikh, which has a temperature of $46°$ C. ($115°$ F.), and lies 270 feet above the Hammet esh Sheikh, or Hammet Selûn of El-Hammi. Seven fine palm trees border the small pond formed by this hot spring, and bathe their roots in the sulphurous waters, which seem to suit their wants exceedingly well. A second hot spring, the Hammet Rîh el-Ghanam, of a temperature of $34°$ C. ($93°$ F.), rises close to the other spring and flows out forming a clear pool of warm water, surrounded by a jungle of cane. Both these hot springs have an outflow of about one cubic metre per second, and are therefore very copious supplies. After watering the palm jungle their waters flow northwards into the Yarmûk.

The 'Ain el-Butmi, and a second small spring called the 'Ain el-Bîr, rise near the huts of Mukhaibi 'Arabs, and water their former fruit gardens, now left to run to waste.

A proper cultivation of the soil, and a judicious storage of the hot and cold springs, would make of El-Mukhaibi and the neighbouring baths of El-Hammi a much-needed sanitary bathing establishment for sufferers of various categories, both from Syria and other lands. The whole region could at present be bought up for but a small price.

A mile and a half down the Yarmûk River, below the hot springs of Mukhaibi, occurs El-Hammi, supposed to be the Roman Amatha, the bathing place of the ancient Gadara. Its hot springs, the theatre, and other ancient remains, with a detailed account and plan of the region, is given in my work already published, by the P. E. F., on "Jaulân."

El Mirdâni es Sôdâ.—A steep mountain spur of basalt rock near El Hammi.

El Hâwiyân and *Hâwit el-'Alu,* are two basalt rocks, between which the Yarmûk has forced its way ; this picturesque rock-gate closes the western extremity of the Yarmûk Valley. The river for a little distance above these rocks is called Sharî'at Abu Kharûf.

El Mezra'a.—Three huts standing among pomegranate and fig plantations, watered by a spring The ten inhabitants of the place belong to Umm Keis.

El-Hareit.—The name of a region in the southern part of 'Arûk ej-Jenânîyeh.

El-Mâssia.—The name of the eastern part of the plain west of Umm Keis.

Es Sbeibi.—The name of part of the valley of the Wâd el-'Arab, near the mouth of Wâd Zahar. It is an extremely fertile spot.

Er Rahwa.—A mountain slope on the Wâd el-'Arab, with traces of ruins in the vicinity.

El-Fakhed.—A small ruin on the hill at the junction of Seil Umm Keis, Wâd el-'Ain, and Wâd-el-Fakhed ; the place was probably built to protect 'Ain Umm Keis, which is situated near it ; the remains, however, are of little importance.

El-Khneizîr.—A ruin of considerable extent below Umm Keis on the slopes bordering the Wâd el-'Arab ; the remains consist of large hewn building stones, traces of foundation walls, &c., and prove its importance in ancient times. The springs in the Wâd el-Khneizîr supplied the site with excellent water.

Ed Dukkâneh.—A terraced mountain slope west of S'ara.

El-Burz.—A ruin of little importance in the stony part of the eastern Siru district, showing traces of walls.

El-Mikyal.—The name of the western extremity

of the Umm Keis plain, so called from the ruin
near this spot.

El-'Ajami. — A ruined Mohammedan shrine,
shaded by two fine terebinths ; large hewn building
stones lie in heaps round the spot, which commands a fine view down into the Wâd el-'Arab.

El-Kabu.—An ancient fortified site, standing
some distance east of Umm Keis. The main ruin
is situated on an eminence, and consists of the
foundation walls of a square temple 97 feet 2 inches
long and 48 feet 7 inches wide, with six columns
forming the gateway to the east. The western
part is divided into several rooms. The columns
are worked in the common limestone found in the
vicinity, and have a lower diameter of 3 feet
10 inches, which is larger than any of the other
columns found at Umm Keis. The column shafts
were in some cases formed of two segments, sometimes of a single block, in either case showing a
square dowel-hole in the centre, $4\frac{3}{4}$ inches across.
Each drum of column shaft had a total length
of from 3 to 5 feet. The bases were of the Attic
order, with a height of 2 feet 6 inches. The
capitals were Corinthian, and about 3 feet in
height. All these remains are so weather-worn
that the style could only be made out in general
lines ; the cornices, however, were better preserved.
The grandeur of the original building may be

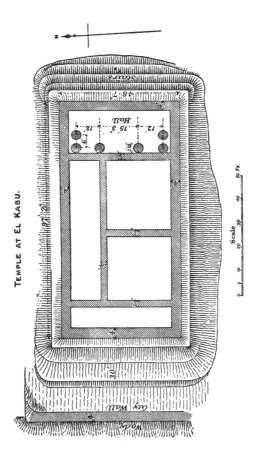

TEMPLE AT EL KABU.

imagined from the fact that the columns, being of the Corinthian order, with a lower diameter of 3 feet 10 inches, had a total height of about 40 feet. The general disposition of the main building of the temple resembles that of the Temple of Fortune in Rome, *i.e.*, Prostyle, the side of which is double the width, and with six columns forming the entrance hall. The extant remains would tend to the conclusion that a stairway originally led from the entrance-hall down to the plateau on which the temple stands.

Thirty feet west of the temple the city wall borders the Wâdy 'Ain el-'Asal. The 'Ain is a fine spring, sufficiently copious to have supplied the ancient city with water. Its overflow runs round three sides of the temple, leaving eastwards a large space of the plateau free for building purposes. The length of the city wall to the east and west is 146 feet, that of the northern and southern half being 390 feet. The construction of this wall is very solid ; it has a width of 4 feet, and is built of large blocks set in mortar.

The site was one that was naturally protected on three sides, since it occupies the summit of a hill spur which falls off abruptly to the east, south, and west, and only on the north is it level with adjacent plateau, where remains are to be seen of a Roman road and aqueduct. On this side there are some traces of a city gate. The other ruins within the wall are of little interest; but the great quantity and the good quality of the hewn basalt and limestone building material, and the large water cisterns, prove the wealth and importance of the city in the past. At present a Bedawîn cemetery occupies the site, and a beautiful Butmi or terebinth, the finest in all the region around, shades a ruined Mohammedan tomb, the name of the person buried therein being now forgotten. Outside the wall to the north I discovered some caves with tombs, of the same arrangement as those described in the survey of Umm Keis.

The situation of El-Kabu among terebinth trees and oaks, and the magnificent view over 'Ajlûn and Jaulân, is worthy of note, and, from the temple ruin, Umm Keis, two miles off, can easily be seen.

Fu'ara.—A small village, built in two separate quarters, containing twenty-six huts, of stone and mud, and numbering a population of about 100 souls. The huts are now in a state of ruin, the villagers are almost starving, and the soil for the greater part lies uncultivated. The cause of this melancholy condition of things is due to the murder, of which the Sheikh, formerly a rich and prosperous man, lies accused. He has now for some time past been imprisoned at Irbid, his property has been

G

confiscated, and the entire population of Fu'ara, all more or less his kinsmen, suffer from the consequences of the Sheikh's crime. It is characteristic of the country how the welfare or the misery of the whole population of a village depends on the Sheikh. If he be rich and esteemed, the villagers are free to act as they please, to take up unclaimed land and acquire property ; if he be poor and in dishonour, the villagers are oppressed and plundered of their rights by any powerful neighbour. The ancient site extends west from the present village, and the ground is covered with ancient building stones. Some stone sarcophagi were seen, also a few ruins overgrown by stunted and ancient olive trees.

Fu'ara has its water from 'Ain Fu'ara, in the Wâdy below, which gives a good and plentiful supply.

Hawwar.—A small village containing twenty-five huts and a population of about 100 souls. The soil is good. The ancient remains are of little interest.

Hâtim.—A village recently rebuilt from the ruins of an ancient site, and at present consisting of thirty poor-looking huts, with a population of 120 souls. The soil is poor.

Ancient building stones are scattered over an area of many acres. In the village itself were found several remains of arched buildings 20 feet long, 15 feet across, and of a rectangular plan, with the upper end built over a cave. The arches were covered with slabs of limestone, and thus recall what is seen in Haurân. The caves we were unable to explore ; they were probably originally mausolea,

ANCIENT BUILDING, HÂTIM.

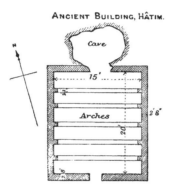

like the building seen near the Western Theatre at Umm Keis. The floors were covered with rubbish, and could not at the time be cleared to make a search for sarcophagi. Besides these arched buildings the ruins of another square building exist, evidently a mosque, measuring 43 feet long from east to west, 14 feet 8 inches from north to south, and having a prayer niche in the southern wall. A pavement beginning at the northern wall leads to the arched entrance.

G 2

At the entrance of a hut a limestone column was found.   The lower face of the base is not parallel with the upper.

COLUMN, HÂTIM.

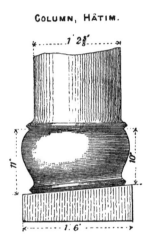

At Hâtim I saw some fine carpets, which are a special industry of Southern 'Ajlûn.   They are made of wool from the sheep of the country, which is dyed at Tiberias, and then woven by the women.   The carpets are called Busât, and are remarkable for their great durability and harmonious colours, which show red, dark blue, green, and sepia bands in alternate rows.   Unfortunately the carpets are not for sale, being made for home consumption only.

The water of the village comes from 'Ain

Hâtim, a spring of moderate supply, in the Wâd el-'Ain.

Ibdar.—A village containing thirty-five tolerably well-built huts of stone and mud, on the southern shoulder of Wâdy Samar, with a population of 150 inhabitants. The village is surrounded by a well grown cactus hedge. A good spring, the 'Ain Ibdar, flows out a little below, to the east, and there are some ancient remains in the neighbourhood.

Jôret el-'Ebâdi.—A hill slope below Khirbet el-Mikyal.

Jôret Sa'id.—A depression in the ground and hill slope near the above.

Khirbet et-Tabak.—A poor looking village of thirteen huts and grain stores belonging to the Bedawîn, who number some 30 souls. For some years past the place has been abandoned in summer time, and is only inhabited during the rainy season. The spring, called 'Ain et-Tabak is of medium supply. Scattered among the huts are some ancient building stones. The situation among the great masses of dark lava is not inviting, but the lands in the Ghôr below are fertile.

Khirbet Mâkûk.—A field covered with large basalt blocks and heaps of hewn building stones, among which grows a terebinth. Traces of rectangular foundation walls exist. The masonry is of the Haurân character, and the site is evidently ancient, and probably goes back to pre-Roman times. The name is, as far as I was able to learn, not Arabic.

Khirbet el-Mikyal.—An ancient site on the Umm Keis plain, covered with scattered basalt building stones. The ploughing of the Fellahîn has nearly destroyed all the remains.

Khirbet Ekseir Hâtim.—Some scattered building stones, cisterns, and unworked limestone blocks on a site belonging to the village of Hâtim (*see* above, page 98).

Khirbet Ekseir Fu'ara.—A place of the same character as the above, with large cisterns, and fig trees growing among the ruins, the property of the village of Fu'ara.

Khirbet Jeharra.—A large ruined site, occupying a commanding mountain ridge above the junction of the Wâd el-Ghafr, the Wâd Barûka, and the Wâd el-'Arab, down which it affords a fine view.

The area covered by the ruins occupy a tract measuring 220 yards of length from east to west, and 160 yards from north to south. Traces of foundation walls exist, and some very large blocks of limestone for building purposes, also some rock-cut cisterns. This once important place is now a complete ruin. An ancient terebinth, the Shejarat

Jeharra, shades the ruins of a Mohammedan tomb, now fallen to decay.

Khallet ed-Dôra.—A hill-slope at Umm Keis.

Khallet et-Tahtanîya, Khallet Huwwâra—Two hill-slopes east of Khirbet Jeharra.

Kefr 'Abâs.—Some scattered building stones, occupying both sides of the high road, with ancient water cisterns in the neighbourhood. Anciently a considerable village.

Kalâ'a es-Sa'âidi.—The name of some large limestone rocks in the Wâd el 'Arab, under which many Bedawîn were buried. (*See* above, page 29.)

Makhâdet el-'Adeisîyeh.—A ford over the Sharî'at el-Menâdireh, or Yarmûk River. It is practicable at all seasons, and lies on the road from Umm Keis to Tiberias.

Rujm el-Menâra.—A small square ruined tower on the Roman high road from Umm Keis to the

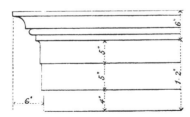

Haurân, situated near Ibdar. Its elevated position, its extraordinarily large and well-hewn building

stones, with the columns and capitals, above which run a cornice and an architrave, would render it probable that we have here either the remains of a small temple or else a watch-tower at the frontier for the collection of toll.   The architrave was divided originally into three parts, with a total height of 14 inches, and the top cornice was 6 inches high.

Parts of a Roman pipe-ornament are also found carved on the stones lying in the ruin. On one of the largest of the building stones, measuring about 2½ feet square, some curious marks or letters were discovered ; they were originally engraved half an inch deep, but are now totally illegible.   It is impossible to say whether this was a Greek inscription or merely a Bedawîn *Wasm*, or tribe mark.

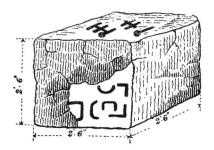

Of the marks here figured, those on the upper

part are doubtless part of a *Wasm*, for the *Dabbûs* ⚲,
or " Club," and the *Shâhid* I, or " Witness," are used
by many Arab tribes, especially the Beni Sakher
of the Ghôr.* Engraving their *Wasm* in a building
signified that they considered themselves the pro-
tectors of the place, and held, as of right, the
Khûwwât, or " brother right," as indemnity for
their trouble.

We found similar marks at other places in 'Ajlûn
and the Ghôr.

Rumeh Fir'ûn, or *El-Hajar el-Maksûr.* — A
broken column shaft, still lying at the limestone
quarry, below Umm Keis on the road to the Jisr
el-Mejâmia.   The shaft, consisting of a single
piece, is 21 feet 10 inches long, and has an upper
diameter of $28\frac{1}{2}$ inches, and a lower of $34\frac{3}{4}$ inches.
An unfinished capital and base are seen at either
end.   In the vicinity many similar column shafts,
of smaller dimensions, 6, 8, and 12 feet long, and
2 feet in diameter, are found, as also large building
stones, which would go to prove that this was the
quarry from which the limestone used in the buildings at Umm Keis was taken.

Sharî'at el-Menâdireh, or the Yarmûk River

* H el Meghzal المغزل and E el-Ehtaâl هلد ل are
Wasms of the 'Akama, عكمة Bedawîn of the tribe of Ja'bna
حمعن

the ancient Hieromax. This important stream the boundary between 'Ajlûn and Jaulân, has been fully described in my surveys published in "Across the Jordan," and " The Jaulân."

Sidd es-Salâibi.—A Wâdy and rock on the lower Sharî'at el-Menâdireh.

Sahl ej-Jûwâni.—A plateau near Malka.

Shejarat el-Fakîri. — A Mohammedan tomb shaded by a tree on the road to the Jordan Bridge above Esh Shûni.

Shejarat el-Beirak, or *Shejarat el-'Arrafîyeh*, also called *Shejarat Barrûka.*—This beautiful terebinth, growing a little to the south of the high road from Umm Keis to the Haurân, has round it traces of ancient ruins. It is a tree of mythic attributes in the common report of the people of northern 'Ajlûn. Its name, Shejarat el-'Arrafîyeh, means "the tree of the seeress," and I was informed that it stands at the place where in ages past kings and warriors used to meet to make peace, or enquire of the seeress as to the future before commencing a war or concluding a peace.

The place seems to have been held sacred since pagan times, and it still maintains in the eyes of the natives a sort of awful sanctity.

Seil Mkeis.—A wâdy with a small brook coming down from Wâd el-'Ain and joining the Wâd el-'Arab above Tell Zara'a.

Sîfîn.—A ruin on the northern slopes of the Wâd el-'Arab. Scattered building stones exist here among the trees.

Sa'ra.—An extensive ruin on the slope called Ed Dukkâneh. Some ruined huts, with large heaps of building stones, and caves and cisterns are found in the neighbourhood.

Samma.—A large village containing eighty huts, and a population of about 350 souls. The huts are tolerably well built of mud and stone. The land in the vicinity is very stony and unfertile. There are few ancient remains.

Sheikh Hutta.—The tomb of a Mohammedan saint, buried beneath a large terebinth near Fu'ara The tree is also called Shejarat Fu'ara.

Sh'eib et-Tahanât.—A road leading to the mills of Wâd el-'Arab, up a gorge south of Khirbet Jeharra.

Tâket el-'Alu.—A basalt precipice and plateau, bordering the Yarmûk gorge at its entrance into the Jordan Valley.

Tell el-Muntâr. — "The watch-tower hill," a small ruined tower on the top of a conical hill at the entrance of Wâd el-'Arab into the Ghôr. Below is the Khirbet el-Muntâr, a site show-ing scattered building remains. The region round about is all called El-Muntâr, and the place from its naturally fortified position may have

served to protect the entrance of the Wâd el-
'Arab.

Umm en-Nakhla.—A hill slope west of Umm
Keis.

Umm el-Khawâbi.—A grave, or possibly a fallen
dolmen, near the road from Umm Keis to the
Jordan Bridge. The place shows several large
hewn blocks of basalt, formerly built together.

Wâd el-'Arab.—This fine valley, the boundary
between the districts of Es-Siru and El-Wustîyeh,
is the great watercourse of Northern 'Ajlûn. The
Wâdy or gorge runs up between the two Nâhiyets
(or Districts) to a spot at a height of about
619 feet above the Mediterranean Sea, and here
bifurcates eastwards to form the important Wâdies
of El-Ghafr and El-Barrûka. Both these are dry
in summer, but the first, rising far in the south-
east, near a place called Hôfa in the Nâhiyet Beni
Juhma, and about 16 miles from its junction with
the Wâdy el-'Arab, gathers an immense amount of
water during the rainy season from all the highlands of 'Ajlûn. The second, the Wâdy el-Barûka,
collects the waters of the eastern Siru, and forms
also a large torrent during the winter rains. From
this point down to its junction with the Jordan in
the Ghôr, the Wâd el-'Arab has a length of about
10 miles, and a difference of level of about 1,480
feet. For the first mile it is dry in the summer,

but below the Khirbet Seidûr is a spring of water
welling out of the white limestone bed ; 800 yards
below this again a second very copious spring
occurs, and further down a number of others
join the stream from both the right and left banks.
The water is clear and good to the taste ; its
amount (in June, 1885) was equivalent to three-
quarters of a cubic meter per second. This
amount is kept up down as far as the junction
with the Wâd Zahar. Here the stream in-
creases to double, and remains at this size until
its entrance into the Jordan Ghôr, where it
rapidly diminishes in volume. The bed of the
stream is everywhere of a soft white limestone,
in which the water has cut small channels, and
thus runs in many parallel streams. The borders
of the wâdy are thickly overgrown with oleander,
cane-brake, and other bushes, which often cover
the stream and the rocks, and overhang the road
which passes through the jungle. In the shallows
formed in the wider parts of the valley excellent
trout are found in great numbers, which are easily
caught. While bathing I was alarmed by seeing
a black water snake, 3 feet long. These are
very much feared by the natives, and, according
to their reports, they are very common in these
streams.

The wâdy gorge is deep and narrow in the

upper part, but gradually widens towards the Ghôr, with green meadows on both banks. Very primitive flour mills are erected in the lower course of the stream, and ruins of more ancient ones are found further up the river. Along the southern bank, below Khirbet el-Bueiri Seidûr, are seen the ruins of water channels and mill buildings, overgrown with bushes and covered with a petrifaction. This petrified mass, according to Dr. Noetling's observation, has been formed by the former hot mineral waters, similar to those found at the baths of El-Hammi, and it would appear from these deposits that the Wâd el-'Arab also formerly contained thermal springs. A gigantic mass of these deposits is found at Tell Zara'a, a hill which rises to a height of nearly 500 feet above the river, and is absolutely covered by these deposits.

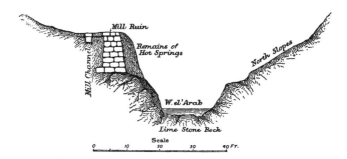

The Wâd el-'Arab is much frequented owing

to the flour-mills, which, with the exception of those found in the Wâdy Zahar, are the only ones worked in Northern 'Ajlun. The Wâd el-'Arab also still remains a favourite hiding place for outlaws and such as have committed crimes, or have some evil purpose in view.

Wâd Samar, Wâd el-Humra, Wâd 'Ain et-Turâb, Wâd 'Ain Ghazal, Nahr Shakk el-Bârid, are the many different names given to the ravine which forms the boundary line between the Districts of Es-Siru and El-Kefarat. The Wâdy rises near 'Ain et-Turâb, at a height of 1,750 feet above the sea, and joins the Yarmûk at a level of 300 feet below the Mediterranean, its length being a little over 10 miles and the total fall 2,050 feet. The gorge is wide in its upper part, and bordered by gentle slopes. It is here called Wâd 'Ain et-Turâb; below it becomes the Wâd Samar and Wâd el-Humra. The wâdy then contracts to a narrow ravine, with high, steep, white limestone cliffs on either bank. For some distance the stream passes at the bottom of a crevice in the plateau but a few feet across, and disappears entirely from view. Below, the wâdy again opens out into a lovely valley, which continues down to its mouth. This lower part is named Nahr Shakk el-Bârid, and at its mouth takes the name of the Wâd 'Ain Ghazâl. A small brook, fed by the numerous springs along its course, runs all the summer through at the bottom of the wâdy. In winter the side ravines and torrents along its banks make this swell to a stream, which cannot be forded without some peril.

Wâd Abu Dmeikh.—A deep ravine, dry in summer, joining the Wâd el-Ghafr below Dokara.

Wâd Mas'aud.—A fine, well-cultivated valley in the Jaulân Province, joining the Yarmûk opposite Wâd 'Ain Ghazal ; for its description *see* " The Jaulân."

Wâd 'Ain et-Tassi.—A narrow ravine opening into the Yarmûk Valley. It is generally dry in the summer months.

Wâd el-Muntamri.—Generally dry in summer. It rises near El-Kabu, and joins the Yarmûk near El-Hammi.

Wâd Mâkûk.—A ravine, dry in summer time, running down from nearly Umm Keis to El-Hammi.

Wâd el-Bareighît.—A ravine, similar to the foregoing, and running parallel to it. Along its slopes caves are met with.

Wâd el-Fakhed.—Dry in summer. It rises at Umm Keis, and joins the Wâd el-'Ain. Along its banks are caves and traces of ruins.

Wâd el-Khneizîr.—The waters from a spring

flow down it, and ultimately join the Wâd el-'Arab.

Wâd el-'Ain.—Dry in its upper course, but bearing a stream in its lower part, where it receives the waters of the 'Ain Umm Keis.

Wâd Bâkûria.—A dry ravine, joining the Wâd Bârûka.

Wâd 'Ain Atîyeh, or *Wâd 'Ain el-Mallâki.*—In part dry, in part bearing a stream which flows from springs. It joins the Wâd el-Humra.

Wâd el-Hadâd.—A dry ravine, beginning near Fu'ara and joining the Wâd el-Ghafr.

Zikel.—A ruin of small importance. Some hewn and unhewn building stones are scattered about the ground over a space of a few acres.

Zôr el-Kusseib.—The name of the lower part of Wâd el-'Arab, near the Ghôr. It consists of a beautifully green meadow, partly covered with cane brake.

CHAPTER IV.

THE DISTRICT OR NÂHIYET EL-KEFARÂT.

The Nâhiyet el-Kefarât is bounded on the north-west and west by the Shari'at el-Menâdireh, or Yarmûk ; on the south by the Nâhiyet es-Siru and the Wâd el-Humra. Its northern and eastern boundaries lie outside the limits of the present Map ; they are formed in part by the District of As Siru, but for the greater distance by the Wâd esh-Shelâleh and the Haurân Province.

The country consists of a plateau, covered in most places by oak forests, and remarkable for its fertile soil, in which it resembles the Haurân plain. Its name recalls the Greek designation of "the Decapolis," for El-Kefarât means the " ruined sites," or " the Villages."

Villages, Ruins, &c., as far as explored.

Arâk el-Heitalîyeh.—A perpendicular precipice of limestone rock, formed by a landslip, bordering the Yarmûk. From the many similar landslips of this vicinity, the Yarmûk Valley in these parts presents an extremely picturesque aspect.

Akhfas el-Heitalîyeh.—A round hill ; a portion

of the above-mentioned 'Arâk. Over it are scattered building stones, probably fallen down from the site above.

'Arakîb el-'Eshshi.—Also a portion of the above-named 'Arâk. It is a steep slope, west of Khirbet el-Heitalîyeh.

'Ain Samar.—A copious spring belonging to the village of Samar.

El-Ehsûn, also called *El-Ekseir, El-Husn,* and *Kala'at el-Husn.* — All these names signify " a castle," or fortified place on a rock precipice. El-Ehsûn is an extensive ancient site occupying the plateau at the summit of an isolated hill, above the Yarmûk. The northern, eastern, and western sides of the mountain fall off abruptly, the highest point rising about 1,100 feet above the Yarmûk Valley, while its southern part is connected by a narrow neck with the mountain ridge bordering the Wâdy Samar. The site shows a great number of large limestone blocks for building, very much weathered, and lying in great heaps. The culminating point of El-Ehsûn was originally occupied by a castle, as seen from the traces of rectangular walls and the great number of building stones piled up there. The position is naturally a very strong one. It commands a wide view over the Yarmûk Valley down to El-Hammi and over a part of Jaulân. To the south and south-west the high mountain

H 2

ridge running between Umm Keis to Ibdar closes the view. Unfortunately neither ornamentations nor inscriptions were discovered to throw light on the origin of this important site. If the identification of Kala'at el-Husn, opposite Tiberias, on the Lake shore (*see* Plan and Description in my Memoir on "Jaulân"), with the Gamala of Josephus, be called in question, the present site of El-Ehsûn may be offered as an alternative site. But the architectural remains found here and its natural position are far inferior to that seen at Kala'at el-Husn of Jaulân. It is impossible at the present day to make out whether or not El-Ehsûn was originally surrounded by a wall.

El-Heitalîyeh.—A small ruin, situated opposite El-Ehsûn above the precipice of 'Arâk el-Heitalîyeh, and connected with the latter site by a mountain ridge. The remains of building stones seen here are of little importance. On the neighbouring slopes, several artificial and natural caves, much fallen in, with some tombs and rock-cut sarcophagi, are found.

El-'Eshshi.—Its name signifies "A nest;" and the site is a hill slope bounded by two wâdies, below El-Heitalîyeh.

El-Ora.—A small plateau above El 'Eshshi.

El-Mar'eiyeh.—A narrow meadow, in the Yarmûk Valley below 'Arâk el-Heitalîyeh.

Halîbna.—An extensive and ancient site on the plateau of the Kefarât, surrounded by oak forests. Remains of rock-cut sarcophagi, cisterns, and caves are seen here. Some of the building stones have a length of 5 feet by 2 feet in height and width.

Helâl el-'Ulleika.—A crescent-shaped slope in the Wâd el-'Ulleika.

Khirbet ed-Deir.—Unexplored. A hill ruin at the head of Wâd 'Ain et-Turâb.

Makhâdet el-Mar'eiyeh.—A ford of the Yarmûk ; both deep and broad.

Makhâdet Umm esh Sherûb and *Makhâdet Umm Kharrûbî.*—Two fords below the above. The first is often used, and is very practicable ; the latter is deep.

Sarîri 'Akrabeh.—A basalt plateau and precipice at the junction of Yarmûk and Rukkâd rivers.

Samar.—A moderate-sized village of 45 huts, built of stone and mud, occupied by a population of 220 souls. Cactus hedges and gardens surround the village, which has its supply of water from a plentiful spring in the wâdy below. The situation is renowned for its view over 'Ajlûn and down into the Wâdy Samar. The people are kindly and hospitable. Few ancient remains are seen here.

Wâdy Kleit.—A large wâdy, with a small perennial stream, during some years running dry in summer. It joins the Yarmûk near the Rukkâd mouth. Here are seen the ruins of an old mill, and in the bed of the Yarmûk below ruins of another, a more modern one, exist, with traces of an ancient mill aqueduct. The upper part of the Wâdy remains unexplored.

Wâd el-'Ulleika.—A wâdy bearing a small brook coming down from *'Ain el-'Ulleika,* a copious spring, halfway up the wâdy bed. At its mouth near the Yarmûk, the Fellahîn of the village of Sahem el-Kefarât have planted some pomegranate gardens. Its upper part remains unexplored.

Wâd el-Ôra.—A small wâdy, with a spring of water which runs down to join the Yarmûk below El-Heitalîyeh.

Wâd Umm el-Karein.—Close to the above; its upper part bifurcates and forms two wide branches. All these above-mentioned wâdies are covered with a growth of brushwood.

Zôr el-Heshra.—A depression and meadow along the Yarmûk, below 'Arâk el-Heitalîyeh.

Zôr en-Nîs.—Below the above: a meadow with traces of ruins, lying on both sides of the Yarmûk.

The other sites and places situated in the Eastern Kefarât remain as yet unexplored.

CHAPTER V.

Nâhiyet el-Wustîyeh.

THE Nâhiyet el-Wustîyeh is bordered on the north by the Wâd el-'Arab, the Wâd el-Ghafr, and the Nâhiyet es-Siru ; on the east by the Nâhiyet Ben Juhma ; on the south by the Wâd et-Taiyibeh and the Nâhiyet el-Kûra ; and on the west by the Ghôr. It lies thus in the midst of the other Nâhiyets, and from this fact its name of El-Wustîyeh (the Middle District) is derived. The north-western portion of the District is a rolling country sloping down to the Wâd el-'Arab, the remainder is a plateau country, intersected by numerous Wâdies and covered with oak wood. The plateau was at one time thickly settled, although its soil is rather poor ; the population is now scanty.

Its principal villages are Kefr Esad and Et Taiyibeh.

Kefr Esad (1,151 feet above the sea.—The

village is nearly on a level with Umm Keis; it is built in two quarters. The southern quarter, numbering twenty huts and containing a population of 100 souls of the families of the " Fukara " or " Shiyûkh " (Fakirs or Sheikhs). The northern quarter consists of some fifty huts, occupied by the Fellahîn and numbers some 250 souls. The " Sheikhs " form a caste apart, considering themselves saints, and excluding from their company the profane Fellahîn of the northern quarter; they are greatly venerated by the latter, and have built themselves a number of miserable huts, in which they live on the revenues afforded by the shrine of a Mohammedan saint called Sheikh Mohammed el-'Udamy. This tomb they carefully attend, and its whitewashed cupola may be seen from many distant parts of Northern 'Ajlûn. The revenues consist of the rent of a mill called " Tâhûnet el-Massadîn," in the Wâd el-'Arab, and other rents drawn from extensive tracts of land called the Jôrt el-Wakif, and from the produce of an olive grove at Er Rumelli, south of the Weli of the Sheikh. The " saints " live in idleness, their huts are covered with mud and dirt, and they do not even keep their linen turbans clean and white, as commanded by the Mohammedan law. They eat up the little property of the villagers in their laziness, and keep the latter in a state of bondage; they hate all foreigners, and, above all, Christians, and I had some difficulty in keeping them from meddling in the affairs of my survey.

The huts of the northern quarter are carefully built with stone, and some few with mud. Some are dry-goods stores. Bee-hives are found in nearly every house yard, the honey being of an excellent quality.

Kefr Esad possesses no spring of water ; it lies on a wide plain, and in its vicinity are a number of ancient cisterns, for the most part covered with a stone slab having a round hole in the centre.

These rock-cut cisterns are of a depth of from 15 to 20 feet, and have an area of from 30 to 80 feet square, some being circular. Circular holes cut in the rocks also served for the smaller troughs; they contain a sufficient supply of tolerably good drinking water, but the neighbourhood of them swarms with mosquitos all the year through. The tract of land where the cisterns are found is called El-Mîdân, and forms the eastern part of the ancient site. To the west of the village are seen the remains of a fallen Jâma', or mosque, measuring 39 feet by 33, with pointed arches, and a paved yard to the north with an entrance gate surmounted by a defaced Koranic inscription. To the west of the Jâma' extends a rocky region named El-

SARCOPHAGUS.
K. ESAD.

Keta'a, where are seen many rock-cut sarcophagi, 7 feet 6 inches long, 1 foot 7 inches wide, and 2 feet deep, also some circular and rectangular wine or oil presses, with steps lead_ing down into them.

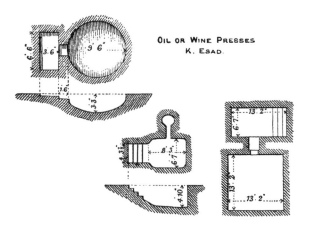

OIL OR WINE PRESSES
K. ESAD.

The other ruins are of little importance. Many ancient stones are found built into the houses, and scattered remains are also found in the adjacent woods.

The Sheikh of Kefr Esad is one of the early settlers in 'Ajlûn who knew the country in the old days when the Bedawîn were lord of all. He is a martial looking man, bears a good character, and is friendly towards foreigners. His breast is covered with scars of sword cuts and lance thrusts ; and when he relates the story of the past his eyes gleam with a wild fire, and the old warrior lives over again the days of his youth. When, however, he looked out over his field and pointed out the Bedawîn 'Arab Sukhûr el-'Alâ, who in the past had ill-treated and tyrannized over him and his relations, but were now peacefully herding his cattle and sheep, he added, somewhat disdainfully, to me, " Massakîn da'ûf elyôm " (but they are all poor beggars now).

Et Taiyibeh (1,283 feet above the sea).—A large and populous village containing 140 well-built huts of stone and mortar, some few of mud, with a population of about 700 souls, among whom there are four Christian families, the remainder being all Mohammedan. Et Taiyibeh formed, not long ago, a separate district, or " Wuzirîyeh," as the natives call it, of its own, independent of El-Wustîyeh. It has of late been curtailed of these rights ; some of its best lands in the Ghôr have passed over to the Kada of Tabarîyeh, and rich proprietors have taken possession of other tracts belonging to the village. Some time ago the villagers rose against their oppressors, and made an attack upon the Pasha of Acre, who during a visit to the Ghôr was put to the rout by a hundred horsemen of their tribesmen and of the allied Bedawîns. He was obliged to flee to Tiberias, leaving as booty to the villagers some of the best bred Arab horses in his stables. The Pasha complained at Damascus, and at present the chieftains of the town are imprisoned there awaiting trial.

Of ancient remains, we found traces of a wall, 3 feet thick, built of huge and well-hewn limestone blocks, also scattered here and there building stones, and some blocks are built into the walls of the houses. Two circular archways, we saw, are evidently of Mohammedan origin, probably the remains of a Jâma', or mosque, similar to the one at Kefr Esad. There is no spring of water near the village, and the drinking water is taken from the storage of ancient rock-cut cisterns, found everywhere in the vicinity. A considerable number of olive trees are planted round the village, and some fig trees and fields of tobacco are also cultivated.

In the extreme east of the village was the 'Ullîyeh, the "upper chamber," a large room in the second storey of an old building, destined for the reception of guests and travellers, and in charge of a Nâtûr, a sort of inn-keeper. Its interior is smoky and dirty, like the other houses, but still preferable to many of the sort of guest-chambers found elsewhere.

Abu en-Namel.—A level tract of country on the southern borders of the Wâd el-'Arab.

Abu Mudawwar.—A small ruin, built on the summit of a hill, near El-Musheirfi.

'Arab Sukhûr el-'Alâ.—A branch tribe of the 'Arab Beni Sakher ; they were, of old, the tyrants of the district, but are now shepherds and herdsmen, and in a dependant position to the villagers. They graze their herds on the plateau of Kefr Esad, and on the southern slopes of Wâd el-'Arab ; they live in about eighty miserable looking hair tents, and number in all scarcely 300 souls.

Ard el-Seidûr.—A tract of land round the site of Seidûr. Traces of ruins, cisterns, and oil presses are found in this plain.

'Ard el-Ghanj.—A slope below Zahar el-'Akabi.

Ard el-Musheirfi.—A wide tract of land west of the ruin of the same name, bearing traces of ruins with scattered blocks of stone, and others laid in rows. Cisterns and caves abound in this neighbourhood.

Ard el-Mahajjeh.—A level tract south of Samma covered with oak trees and Dolmens, partly fallen, partly standing (*see* El-Ekla'a el-Mutrakibât, p. 131).

'Arkûb el-Hummad.—A hill slope below Kôba' south of Wâd el-'Arab.

'Arkûb el-Emessakhîn.—A hill-slope south of the above. On its upper part are the so-called 'Ahjâr el-Emessakhîn (?) pointed and rounded stones, forming a hard mass of concrete, in balls, which lie embedded in the softer limestone rock.

They border the road coming up from from Tell Zara'a to Kefr Esad, and lie in rows or scattered over the plain. The Arab legend asserts that they were formerly human beings. "Two women, it is said, travelling with their children, stopped at this place and had unlawful intercourse with merchants passing by on the same road. For their penance, God Almighty transformed them into stones." This story is well known and believed throughout the whole vicinity.

'Arâk ez-Zutt.—A slope on the Wâd el-Amûd below Kefr Esad.

'Arâk er-Râhib.—The upper southern slope of the Wâdy Zahar.

'Arâkîb es-Sâkhui.—The hill slopes of the western Wustîyeh, bordering the Ghôr, intersected by numerous small watercourses.

'Ain es-Smeirât.—A small spring of poor water

supply on the borders of the Wâd el-'Arab, entirely overgrown by bushes.

'Ain el-Kirkâsi.—A spring with a good supply of water on the borders of Wâdy Zahar.

'Ain el-'Abhara.—A small spring flowing into the Wâd el-'Arab.

'Ain Mendah.—The spring with a good supply of water, flowing out at the village of the same name.

Bersînia.—A ruined site, which, owing to its extensive remains, is one of the most important spots on the present Map. The ruin is bounded on the north by the Wad el-Mahwara, on the west and south by another small watercourse, while to the east extends the level plain. It thus occupies a sort of projecting tongue of land, and the remains cover an area of 450 yards in length from west to east, and of about 300 yards from south to north.

The immense quantities of hewn building stones with weathered cornices found here, with the heaps of squared stones, the traces of buildings, caves, and deep cisterns, partly built up, and partly hewn out of the rock, with the fragments of limestone troughs 5 feet in length, and 1 foot in depth and width, all go to prove the importance of this site in ancient times, though the ruins are now so weather-worn that no plans could be drawn. At the extreme east, where the ground, which has

its highest point in the centre, slopes down to the
level of the plateau, I found distinct remains of a
city gate. Several limestone lintels were lying
here, measuring each 8 feet in length, and 3 feet
in height, with holes in them to receive the

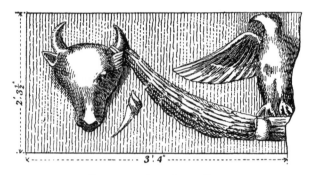

REMAINS OF CITY GATE, BERSINIA.

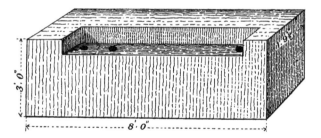

hinges of à stone gate. A square stone, broken
across, had cut on it the head of an ox, much
defaced, with a wreath and an eagle with out-
spread wings in the centre, next to which was a
kind of torch.

A similar ornament was found at Al Ahmedîyeh (*see* "Jaulân," page 72). The highest point of the site, in the centre of the ruins, had evidently been crowned by a building of strong character. The western part is now occupied by the remains of some huts, which may have been built about a century ago. There are also some other remains near the cisterns. It seems probable that the site was originally surrounded by a fortified wall, although the line cannot now be clearly traced. Outside, that is east of the gate, some scattered ruins are again found.

The name "Bersînia" is, as far as I know, not Arabic, and the remains betray a Roman origin. A spring gushes out near the southern boundary, but generally runs dry in summer.

I regret not having been able to spend time in making excavations at this site, and I was unable to make my way into the caves, a work which would doubtless repay the labour of removing the *débris* now choking their entrances.

Dmeikh es-Sreij.—A hill slope on the southern borders of Wâd el-Ghafr.

Dhaher el-Ahmâr.—A mountain shoulder between two wâdies, near Tell Zara'a.

Dhaher ed-Deir, or *Abu'l Harct.*—A hill near Deir es-Sa'neh, the top of which is covered with ruins.

I

Deir es-Sa'neh, or *Ed Deir.*—A small village containing twenty miserable huts, built of stone, and mud ; the population of 100 souls are mostly immigrants from Jebel Nâblus, who came hither but few years ago. Of ancient remains, several vaulted buildings exist, one of which was a *Jâma'*, or Mosque, showing a prayer niche in the south, with a defaced Koranic inscription, and some small limestone columns. Outside the village are seen the remains of rock-cut sarcophagi and cisterns. On the east are some orchards of pomegranate and fig trees, and an olive grove. To the south-west an ancient oak, or *Mallûli,* shades the remains of the Mohammedan Weli Abu'l Kâsem ; and south of this again is El-Birket, a depression in the ground filled by a pool measuring 50 yards by 30, which is overgrown with marsh plants.

The *Tell ed-Deîr* is a terraced hill lying to the east of the village, which ten years ago was covered with fig plantations. The eastern end slopes abruptly down into the Wâd el-Emgharîyeh. The plateau measures but 120 feet across in either direction, and is covered with large heaps of carefully hewn building stones, with a Bedawîn grave-yard in between. The hill was originally fortified, and traces of a wall can still be recognised. Several terraces are hewn out some 30 feet apart, each of them having a retaining wall.

Ed Deir must have been a site of considerable importance, since the whole area between the chief ruins, the Tell and Birket, is covered with traces of ancient remains.

Bersînia, which lies near it on the east, belongs to Ed Deir.

Darb el-Ekfûl.—The main road from the Jisr el-Mejâmia' across the Wustîyeh and Beni Juhma Districts to Irbid and Southern Haurân. To judge from its pavement the road is of Roman origin.

El-Halfawîyeh.—A level tract and hill-slope east of Tell Zara'a.

El-Kelkhiât.— A hill-slope, or rather a range of small hills, forming part of the Wâd el-'Arab, near the Ghôr.

El-Keta'a.—A tract of flat land lying south-west, and

El-Mîdân.—A similar plain lying north-east of Kefr Esad.

El-Eklâ'a el-Mutrakibât.— A Dolmen field on the Ard el-Mahajjeh, south of Samma, and north of Et Taiyibeh. In the one Dolmen, still intact, the two side stones have a length of 11 feet 5 inches and 11 feet 9 inches, and a height of 2 feet 7 inches to 3 feet. These Dolmens were set up nearly due west and east. A third stone is fitted in between the two side stones on the west, but no head-stone is found in the east quarter. A large

I 2

slab, 11 feet 9 inches in length, and from 5 feet

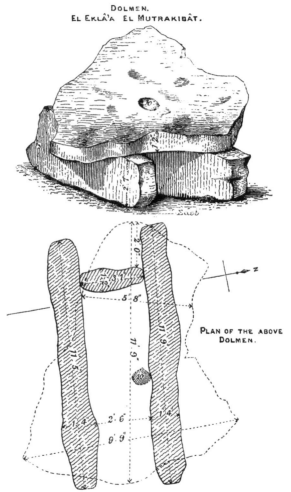

DOLMEN.
EL EKLÂ'A EL MUTRAKIBÂT.

PLAN OF THE ABOVE
DOLMEN.

8 inches to 9 feet 9 inches across, and 1 foot

2 inches thick, generally covers the entire Dolmen. The space left in the interior of the Dolmen has a width at the west end of 3 feet 1 inch, and narrows to 2 feet 6 inches at the eastern end. The covering slab shows in its centre a depression, like a round hole, some 10 inches in diameter, and 4 inches in depth. The stones and slabs are of the limestone formation found in the vicinity, and were probably quarried somewhere in the Wâd Samû'a, where similar slabs may still be found. There were apparently twelve Dolmens originally in this field, but all, with the exception of the one described, are now fallen to ruin, and being constructed of the soft limestone, are less well preserved than the basalt Dolmens found in north-western Jaulân.

The Ard el-Mehajjeh is now well cultivated, and these ancient remains disappear every year more and more.

Walking along the road from here towards Et Taiyibeh some remains of other Dolmens were found ; and at the little elevation called Jelamet Shômar, half way between Samma and Et Taiyibeh, a few side slabs are still *in situ*. Similar traces are found all along the road from Zebda to Et Taiyibeh.

It may therefore be concluded that the country along the Wâd Ibsarr, from near Samma as far as

Taiyibeh, was anciently occupied by a field of Dolmens, stretching for a length of two miles, and having a width of half a mile. The Dolmens found in the Nâhiyet Beni Juhma (*see* below, page 169) were in better preservation to those just described.

El-Meshrîyeh.—The name of the hill slope near the Arâk er-Râhib.

El-Musheirfi.—A ruin on the shoulder of the mountains above Darb el-Ekfûl. A few ruined huts and fireplaces prove that the spot was not long ago inhabited. The caves seen in the vicinity are mostly fallen in, and seem to have been similar in plan to those of Umm Keis, with loculi and sarcophagi. The highest point of the site, called El-Kenîseh (or the Church), is built round with large stones, forming a rectangular building 60 feet square, some of the stones having a length of 5 feet and a height and width of 2 feet. These are worked in bosses, as the annexed sketch indicates.

The walls have a width of 5 feet and more. South of the Kenîseh some other remains of buildings exist, also a few cisterns.

The extent covered by the ancient site is not very considerable ; but the position was a strong one, and it would seem as though El-Kenîseh originally formed the castle, being protected by two wâdies on either side, and commanding a fine view over the Wâd el-'Arab, and its tributaries in the wide plains to the. west. El-Mesheirfi lies immediately opposite Umm Keis, the latter occupying the northern shoulder, and El Meshierfi the southern high lands of the Wâd el-'Arab.

A spring of moderate supply, the 'Ain Ummerkâ, wells up in the bed of the western wâdy, which is named after it.

Freika'.—A small ruin in the Ghôr, occupying a small hill. Unexplored.

Hôfa.—A clean and neatly built village, containing 50 stone-built huts, plastered with a white clay, with a population numbering about 350 souls. Among them are two Christian families. The entrances into the Shiekh's yard are surmounted with stone lintels, carefully worked with a modern ornamentation and texts from the Koran.

Of ancient remains are traces of walls, 4 feet 5 inches thick. The Weli in the east is that of the Mohammedan Sheikh Sa'id. Several cisterns and caves exist in the neighbourhood. Olives, pomegranates, figs, and grapes are cultivated in the orchards, and vegetables are raised in the neighbourhood of the village.

A little way from the town are found oil presses, similar to those at Kefr Esad.

Jôrt el-Wakif.—A tract of country near Kefr Esad, belonging to the Weli of Sheik Muhammedh el-'Udamy.

Jîjîn.—A miserable village of 20 huts, but situated in a fertile country. There are few ancient remains. The population consists of about 80 souls.

Jelâmet Shômar.— A tract of land near Et Taiyibeh, showing remains of a Dolmen field.

Ibsarr.—A ruin of some extent, now overgrown by the ancient oak forest. Traces of walls exist, and heaps of hewn building stones.

Khirbet el-Bueiri Seidûr.—A ruin on the southern slopes of Wâd el-'Arab. Its remains are of little interest. There are ruins of a mill on the river below.

Khirbet el-Bueiri.—An unimportant ruin, on a small hill near Wâdy Zahar.

Khirbet el-'Askalânî.—The ruin of a Weli of a Mohammedan saint, standing in a fine oak forest.

Khirbet es-Sâkhni.—A small ruin on the borders of the Ghôr.

Khirbet Hasân.—A ruin of small extent near Wâd Samû'a. Heaps of building stones lie near it.

Kefr 'An.—A ruin of some importance on the Wâd el-Mehwara, or Wâdy Kefr 'An. Traces of ancient vaulted buildings and heaps of hewn stones lie about on every hand. Unfortunately I had not sufficient leisure for a thorough examination of the site.

Kôba.—A mountain shoulder jutting out west of Seidûr.

Kefr Rahta.—A village of moderate size, with tolerably well built stone and mud huts, numbering 40 in all, with a population of about 200 souls. Some ancient remains lie round the village.

Kharâi.—A ruin, with scattered building stones, on the Wâdy Kharaj, now overgrown by the oak forest.

Kamm.—A ruin on the main road of Darb el-Ekfûl. Its remains crown a small elevation, about 200 yards square, and it must once have been an important place. The walls still standing have a thickness of 3 feet 3 inches, the hewn building stones, of which there are quantities lying about, are large, and in parts bossed. To the south the ruins of a Jâma', Mosque, are found, and some large rock-hewn cisterns.

Kumeim.—A moderate sized and poor village, containing 40 huts of mud and badly-built masonry, with a population of about 200 souls. The remains of old walls extend southwards, but are of little interest. In the village itself was found an ancient vaulted building, now fallen in, 30 feet long, 20 feet wide, with a rectangular niche in the southern wall, evidently the remains of a Mosque.

The masonry work is very rough. In its vicinity some rock-hewn cisterns exist, but no spring of water. Some ancient olive trees grow in the neighbourhood.

Khallet Khalaf.—A hill slope below Seidûr.

Khallet el-Beduwîyeh.—A finely wooded slope west of Seidûr,

Khallet Abu'l Lôz.—A hill slope of the Wâdy Zahar and of the Wâd el-'Amûd, covered with wild almond trees. It is said that the entire region west of and below Zahar el-'Akabi, was once planted with almond trees, and hence the name " Abu'l Lôz," which signifies the " Place of Almond Trees."

Khallet Sbeih.—A hill slope below Khirbet el-'Askalâni.

Khallet Abu Halâl. — A horseshoe-shaped hill slope east of Et Taiyibeh.

Khallet el-Ehreish.—A hill slope south of the above, with traces of ancient vineyard walls along it.

Moyet et Taltamisîyeh.—A small wâdy watered by a perennial spring. It joins the Wâd el-'Arab at Tell Zara'a.

Mendah.—A miserable-looking village, containing 42 mud and stone huts, with a population of about 200 souls. West of the village is a spring, with a good water supply, also an ancient olive grove. There are few ancient remains.

Mukraba.—A well built village, containing 45 huts and about 250 inhabitants. The huts are well constructed and large. The inhabitants are immigrants from Jebel Nâblus, and, as I was informed by their Sheikh, Diâb, they are all members of one family, and nearly related one to another. They are very laborious, and cultivate some lands in the Ghôr. The women keep bees, and excellent honey is produced. They have also some tobacco planted round the manure heaps of the village. The reception of the guest and his entertainment by the Nâblus people is very different from what is met with in other villages in 'Ajlûn. The visitor can never reckon on the hospitality so willingly offered by the Fellahîn and Bedawîn Arabs. Among the Nâblus immigrants it is clearly felt to be merely a forced adoption of a custom of the country in which they have settled.

Of ancient remains there are, in the eastern part of the town, the ruins of a vaulted Jâma', or Mosque. North and south of the village are scattered building stones, with rock-cut cisterns and caves. A little to the north, on a stony hill, some traces of walls and sarcophagi are found. The sarcophagi are cut in the limestone rock, and have a length of from 6 to 7 feet, by 2 feet in width and 3 in depth. They are covered by slabs 4 feet wide, 9 feet long, and 1 foot to 1 foot 6 inches thick.

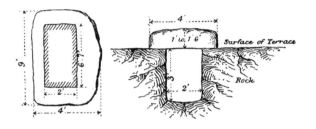

A number of these sarcophagi lie yet unopened, and the people would not allow of our searching their interiors.

This northern hill covered with remains appears to be the ancient site of Mukraba. Its extent would prove it once to have been an important place.

The village suffers for lack of water, as the cisterns do not suffice for the consumption, and no good spring is found near. From the latter half of June, therefore, the women are obliged to go for their household water supply to the Wâdy Zahar, which, in its nearest point, is over two miles distant from the village, and the road is more than bad all the latter part of the way.

Râs Wâd Zahar.—About a dozen springs, overgrown with cane and oleanders, which form the head waters of the Wâd Zahar.

Sâhel ed-Deir.—A level tract of country west of Deir es-Sa'neh.

Samma.—A large and well built village. containing 55 huts, mostly built of stone ; with a population of over 300 souls. The people are friendly to strangers. Many ancient cisterns are kept carefully cleaned, and contain sufficient rain water for the supply of the village. Some olive groves, tobacco gardens, and rows of bee-hives are seen in the vicinity. The ancient remains are of little importance. West of the village the ruined Mohammedan Weli er-Refâ is pointed out.

Seidûr.—A large and important ruin, on the southern bank of Wâd el-'Arab. The remains cover an area of 300 yards square, occupying a sloping tract of ground looking down into the valley of the Wâd el-'Arab, and across it to Umm Keis. Its commanding position, with the great quantities of building stones and broken architectural fragments, the many large cisterns and the caves now filled up with rubbish, prove the ancient importance of the site. Unfortunately all the architectural remains are now so much weather-worn that they could not be sketched ; the only stones that remained intact were the so-called " Roman pipes." Many " Mallûl " oaks shade the ruin.

Sôm.—A medium-sized village, sparsely built, of 40 huts of mud and stone ; some of which show careful masonry and mortared joints. The population is about 200 souls. Few ancient remains are seen. West of the village is the shrine called the Weli Abu Derda, which is carefully maintained by the villagers. On the north is the Wâd el-Ghafr.

Tell Zara'a.—A nearly circular hill in the lower part of the Wâd el-'Arab. Its northern part falls perpendicularly off into the river bed, and forms a high precipice, which is coated with the sediment of former hot springs. In the centre of the hill plateau, which measures about 150 yards in every direction, and occupying a small depression, is a spring, which rises in the middle of a small pond, almost overgrown with high cane jungle. The water flows down the slopes of the Tell into the Wâd el-'Arab. The Bedawîn of the neighbourhood, as well as the Fellahîn, say that the water was originally hot, and that it had a salt and sulphurous taste ; at the present day the water is perfectly sweet ; but Dr. Noetling's examination confirms the account that the spring was formerly hot, and also sulphurous in character.

A strong wall in old days surrounded the hill, and near the spring, as well as a little to the south of it, we found remains of rectangular buildings the walls of which were composed of enormous hewn blocks of limestone and basalt. The culminating point of the hill plateau is occupied by the remains of a strong building. Round the eastern slope of the hill a channel may still be seen, which led the water across the southern part of the ruin. The hill is isolated in position, being surrounded on all sides by the steep Wâdies.

Tell el-Kâk.—A small hill at the junction of Wâd Zara's and Wâd el-Amûd.

Tell es-Seirawân.—A small hill with some ruined buildings on the borders of the Ghôr.

Tell ed-Deir. — Ruins. (*See* Deir es-Sa'neh, p. 130.)

Tâhunet el-Ersân, Tâhunet el-Emheidât, Tâhunet el-'Azzâm, Tâhunet el-Messadîn, Tâhunet el-Menshîyeh, Tâhunet el-Ahsûn, Tâhunet el-Matlak el-Ahsein, Tâhunet el-Beshâiri, Tâhunet ed-Dueikât, Tâhunet Sa'ûd 'Azzâm, Tâhunet Umm Dâlieh, Tâhunet Mazeid Effendi, Tâhunet el-'Arîd, Tâhunet el-Kleï'ât.—These fourteen mills are situated on or near the brook of the Wâd Zahar. They generally possess but one millstone a-piece and are of a very primitive construction, but being the only corn mills in this part of the country they are always in work, and would, under a better system, pay their owners an exceedingly handsome profit.

Umm el-Ghuzlân.—A ruin covering an area of about four acres, but showing no remains except scattered stones and some ancient cisterns. An abundant growth of oak trees covers the area.

Umm Hanna.—A small ruin on the main road of Darb el-Ekfûl. The place is called by some Mhanna, but I imagine the first to be the more correct spelling.

Umm Erkâ'a.—A depression of land and a slope below El-Musheirfi.

Wâd el-Ekseir.—The lower part of the Wâd el-'Arab. It is a fine valley and stream, with fertile slopes on the borders.

Wâd el-Halfawîyeh. — A small stream in a wâdy which joids the Wâd el-Arab east of Tell Zara'a.

Wâd el-Amûd.—(1.) A wide wâdy, which rises at Kefr Esad and joins the Wâd Zahar near Tell el-Kâk. No perennial stream runs down it, but good pastures lie along its slopes and the soil is fertile. The main road down to the mills of Wâd Zahar passes along this valley, and is bordered by an abundant growth of different kinds of brushwood.

(2.) A wâdy of the western part of the Wustîyeh, rising at the Khallet es-Sbeih. It is very rocky. There is no stream in its upper part. Its lower part, in the Ghôr, still remains unexplored.

Wâd Zahar.—This fine stream is the most important tributary of the Wâd el-'Arab. It rises at Râs Wâd Zahar, below Zahar el-Akabi, from which it takes its name. At its upper end it has a height of about 260 feet above the Mediterranean, and joins the Wâd el-'Arab close by Tell Zara'a at a level of about 60 feet below the sea level. Its total fall is therefore 320 feet, in a length of only 3 miles. At the points where the high road crosses the river the stream had a width (in June, 1885) of 14 feet and a depth of 10 inches, its waters being clear and of an excellent quality. During its rapid course it works the fourteen flour mills already mentioned (p. 143). The banks are abundantly overhung with oleanders, raspberry bushes, and cane-brake. Small natural ponds occur, which are full of fish, and a refreshing bath, an exceptional luxury in Northern 'Ajlûn, can be taken in them by the dusty traveller.

Little above the Râs (or head waters), where many springs gush out from the surrounding slopes, the wâdy bed divides up into several ravines. The principal of these is the Wâd Kharaj, further up called Wâd Shômar, and which rises in the district of El-Kûra, but carries no water in summer.

K

Wâd Kumeim.—A small wâdy, rising at the village of the same name ; it is dry in summer. Near Hôfa it is called Wâd Hôfa, and it joins Wâd Samma a little below this.

Wâd Abu Sarâj.—A gorge rising at Kamm and joining the Wâd Kumeim. It is dry in summer.

Wâd Sammâ.—The upper part of the Wâd Kharaj (*see* Wâd Zahar).

Wâd Shômar.—The upper part of the Wâd Samma. It forms part of the boundary between El-Wustîyeh, Beni Juhma, and El-Kûra. This important tributary of the Wâd Zahar rises in the Nâhiyet el-Kûra. It is wide and deep, is sometimes rocky and sometimes fertile, and alternately wooded and bare. Although dry in summer in winter the torrent is considerable.

Wâd Ibsarr.—A tributary of the above, and also dry in summer. Its upper part is called the Wâd el-Emgharîyeh; also dry, and of little importance.

Wâd el-Bîreh. — A rocky, steep wâdy, being perfectly barren and dry. It rises west of Mukhraba, and falls into the Ghôr.

Wâd Zebda.—Rises near Zebda, and joins the above. It is dry in summer, and but a small gorge.

Wad et Taiyibeh.—This important wâdy, also known as Wâdy Jenîn and Wâdy Samûa, is the boundary between El-Wustîyeh and El-Kûar. It rises in the latter Nâhiyeh, and is called Wâdy es-Sheil, at a place called Ehdeija. Only a part of its course is marked on the present Map. Near Samû'a its bed, dry in summer, has a depth of about 500 feet below the surrounding plateau country. Its borders are very rocky ('Ajlûn marble). It is very steep, and the stream is difficult to ford in winter. The bed is luxuriously overgrown with shrubs of *'Abhar* or *Lubna* and oak-scrub. Its upper slopes are covered with ancient vineyard-walls, and traces remain of small watch houses, built up of the huge blocks with which the vicinity abounds.

Zahar el-'Akabi.—A ruin and a ruined village, still inhabited a year ago. The ancient building stones are found spread over a wide area, and many are built into the now ruined huts of the modern villagers. No remains of interest could be discovered, although the place, according to tradition, was once of importance.

Zebda.—A miserable village, of ten huts and about 40 inhabitants. The soil is poor, and the Fellahîn seem to be on the point of abandoning the place. Many ancient stones, some cisterns, and ancient olive trees are found in the neighbourhood.

K 2

CHAPTER VI.

Nâhiyet Beni Juhma.

The area of this Nâhîyet is only partly included in the present Map. Its western part is bounded by the Districts of Es-Siru and El-Wustîyeh ; its southern by El-Kûra ; its eastern by the Haurân ; and its northern again by the Nâhiyet es-Siru. The district occupies a sloping country, having its highest point in the south, in the Jebel 'Ajlûn, from whence it slopes towards the Wâd el-Ghafr. There is a high plateau again to the east beyond Irbid and Beit Râs, from whence the country slopes towards this same wâdy. The western lands of the district are very little fertile, but the eastern part, in the plain of El-Bukâ'a and the adjacent country to the northward, is almost as fertile as the Southern Haurân country. No large stream is found on the portion figured on the present Map, and to judge from the great reservoirs of the ancient inhabitants found at Irbid and Beit Râs this waterless condition existed in very ancient times. The whole country is perfectly bare of forest or trees.

Principal villages are Irbid, Beit Râs, and Kefr Yûba.

Irbid.—1,733 feet above the sea. The seat of the Kada of Irbid or 'Ajlûn, and the residence of the Kaimakâm, or Lieutenant-Governor.

The village contains about 130 houses and huts, some of them being sufficiently well built. The population is said not to exceed 700 souls. The Serâya, or Governor's house, is a double-winged building, surrounding a large court-yard, and lays claim to no architectural advantages. It is quite modern, and was built to supply the most urgent needs of the officials. Other small Government buildings situated near it are of no importance. A " sûk," or market, is found in the south of the town, and some shops for supplying the requirements of the Fellahîn in the matter of dry goods and groceries are found in the town. South of the village, on the high road coming from the Ghôr and going through Irbid to the Haurân, the Government has constructed two large water reservoirs for the public use. The eastern tank is evidently ancient, it measures 55 feet by 38 feet, and into this the rain water is at first led in order to be cleared. It is thence conducted to the second and modern basin, measuring 90 yards in length,

50 yards in width, and 13½ feet deep. The tanks are surrounded by walls of 4 feet 3 inches in thickness. Several steps lead down to the surface of the water, in order to facilitate the filling of jars, &c. Near the tank were several ancient sarcophagi of basalt with a wreath ornamentation, now used as troughs for cattle. A large cistern near, watched by a guard of soldiers, is destined to supply drinking water for the use of the Government officials. A second guard is set to prevent the Fellahîn women and herdsmen from misusing the waters of the two basins, for in other parts of the country it is customary to wash clothes and take a bath in the wells or basins whence the drinking water is obtained. On the 5th June, 1885, the large basin had 5½ feet of water in it, which was said to be a sufficient supply to last until the rainy season returned. With the exception of this Birket (or tank) Irbid has no other water, and in making this the seat of Government it was their first duty to ensure a sufficient supply of this necessary of life.

The town is built on the southern slope of an artificial hill, the plateau of which is occupied on the south side by a *Kala'a* (or castle), built by Senân Pasha, some score of years ago. Although it is so modern it is already falling to decay, and is no longer tenanted. A southern gateway with a pointed arch leads into a square courtyard, enclosed by buildings containing rows of vaults built of limestone and basalt ; but the building stones are small and the mortar is of bad quality. From the yard several now ruined stairways lead up to the original second storey, of which some few remnants remain on the southern side. The entire building measures outside 178 feet in every direction, the first storey having a height of 21 feet 5 inches. The vaults are used by the shepherds for their flocks, and in the winter sometimes by the soldiers also. The hill seems to have formed the most important part of the ancient site ; it is of a square or rather oblong shape, extending in the length nearly due north to south. It was originally fortified by a triple wall running around the edges of the plateau and round the slopes. The lines can now no longer be distinctly traced, but the construction seems to have been of huge blocks laid irregularly and without mortar.

West of the hill, towards El-Bariha, other remains of an ancient character were discovered.

In the interior of the city is a well-preserved and ancient mosque. A fine spiral staircase is still standing in it, and several basalt sarcophagi with wreath and lion-head ornamentations lie about in the courtyard, where some ancient cisterns are to be seen. Above the entrance to the Makâm (or shrine) of the Mohammedan Saint, Sheikh Sa'ad, several ancient lintels of the Haurân character are noticeable, with wreath ornamentation, rosettes, and animals' heads ; these, however, have all been more or less defaced by fanatic hands.

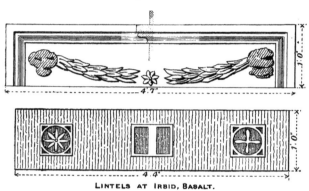

LINTELS AT IRBID, BASALT.

At the centre of Irbid, not far from the Mosque, is an ancient mausoleum, still tolerably well preserved, and now inhabited by an old woman. On the south side is a rectangular entrance, 2 feet 9 inches wide, 4 feet 5 inches high, with cornices and a wreath ornament, containing the inscription :—

The interior of the mausoleum consists of a circular

vault 18 by 16 feet wide; the building stone is limestone, well hewn, and, as far as one could see, set in mortar. The joints, however, are now split open, as seen in the annexed sketch, and are from ⅛ to ½ an inch wide. To the right hand of the door a small square hole which served to hold the lock, similarly to that at the Umm Keis mausoleum.

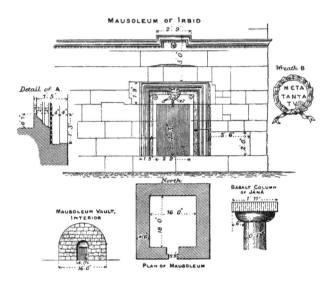

The remains at Irbid are of the Haurânian character, with reference both to the ornamentation and to the basalt stone used there, which was absent elsewhere throughout Northern 'Ajlûn, except only at Umm Keis. From the Kala'a or castle the view embraces the whole of that part of the Decapolis which we had just explored, and extends over the fertile plain of El-Bekâ'a, which is crossed by the camel caravans going to the Haurân. The only drawback to the place is the want of water, otherwise Irbid would soon become a town of equal importance with Sheikh Sa'ad in the Haurân, the climate and soil, as well as the central position, being all that can be desired.

Irbid is always considered to represent the ancient Arbela a city of the Decapolis—not to be confounded with the other Arbela (also called Irbid by the Muslims) of Galilee, near Tiberias. The ancient inscriptions, fragments of which are still found, have all been defaced by the Arabs, and one, evidently of Christian origin, in the yard of the mosque, had been almost totally destroyed.

Beit Râs (1,931 feet above the sea).—A poor-looking village, containing but thirty-five inhabited huts, with a population of about 170 souls. With the exception of Tibneh this is the highest inhabited place on the present Map. The hill on which the village is built, and which, from its wide view and commanding position, is a most conspicuous object throughout this part of the country, is called the Tell el-Khudr, after El-Khudr (St. George), whose shrine or Weli is built on the western slope of the mountain. This is a small

Plan of
BEIT RÂS
sketched by
G. SCHUMACHER, C.E.
1885.

Ard es Stâvia

Road (Sultâni) to Harûna.

Tell el Milh

Ruins

To Kefr-Jâiz

To Tukbul

To Tukbul

To el Bâriha

To el Bâriha and Irbid.

To el Bâriha and Irbid.

'Tell el Kinda'

El Whide

Birket

Columns

Marble

El Emtâkka

Oak

Oak

Oak

Moslem Cemetery

Village.

Jâma'

Ruins

Ruins

Jâma' Birket

Ruins

Bir Abu

Umdân

Cave Bir-Umm el Ghuzlân

R O M A N   R O A D

To Maru.

Sudge ed-Damari.

Caves

Ruins

Khel Miâan.

To Habama.

To Sâl.

Sultâni to Irbid.

Caves

Ruins

ROMAN ROAD

Scale of Feet

0   100   200   300   400   500

F. Weller, lith

square building, with a cupola and Koranic inscriptions running round it, and fragments of ancient
columns, &c., built into the walls. The shrine of
El-Khudr is venerated by both the Moslems and
the Christians of the neighbourhood. Crosses and
Mohammedan emblems are painted over the outside
of the building with "henna," a dye of a reddish
colour. Khudr el-Abbâs (the "Green Saint"), is a
mysterious personage, much venerated all over
Palestine, and is identified with Mâr Irius of the
Christians.

From the shrine of El-Khudr a steep slope leads
to the small plateau of Tell el-Khudr ; the plateau
is surrounded by the ancient city wall, which does
not, however, include the shrine of El-Khudr,

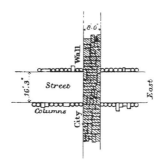

but running along the western border of the
plateau, turns southwards down the slopes and
eastward up to the main street, which, as at Umm
Keis, runs through the middle of the site, and is

the high road to the Haurân.   From the point
where the wall crosses the main street, and where
it has a thickness of 8 feet, it takes a short northern
bend, and then a western direction, going zigzag
up the slopes of the terraced wâdy, until it rejoins
the point whence it started on the plateau.   The
ancient city wall thus encloses an area of about
fifty-one acres: the height of the wall and the stones
used in its construction varying with the position.
The building stones are limestone for the core, and
basalt for the exterior, and are of a large size and
carefully hewn.   The paved street, which apparently
commenced at a gate in the interior of the city, is
bordered by column shafts, as at Umm Keis, and
has about the same width, namely, 16 feet 3 inches.
It can be followed for nearly two miles east of the
city in the direction of Maru.   The gate in the
interior of the town shows remains of a double-
arched gangway, each arch having a width of
16 feet 3 inches; there are remains of a richly-
ornamented architrave, and an eagle is sculptured
on each of the two keystones, which now lie fallen
upside down on the street below.   The ornamentation is unfortunately very much weather-worn, the
building stone being the soft and crumbling-limestone.   Great hewn stones measuring 4 feet by 3
lie round the gateway, bearing defaced inscriptions,
of which a paper squeeze gave no legible result.

No signs of a gate at the east end of the city were discovered.

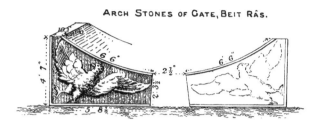

ARCH STONES OF GATE, BEIT RÂS.

Close to the main street, in the interior of the town, are the remains of a Jâma', or Mosque. It is a square building, 78 feet long from east to west, and 43 feet 2 inches wide, divided in the width

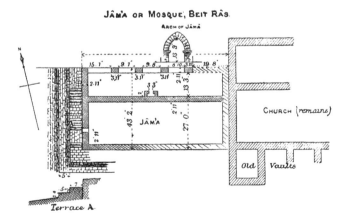

JÂM'A OR MOSQUE, BEIT RÂS.

into two naves, the northern of which has a prayer-

niche in the southern wall.   The north façade has
arcades with pointed arches, of which but one yet
remained intact, the others, as also the walls of
the Mosque, being now almost entirely ruined.

The pillars of the arcades are composed of
carefully-hewn stones with open joints—a form
peculiar to 'Ajlûn—and a simple cornice above;
the mortar used is of good
quality.

ARCADE PILLAR OF
JÂMA.

To the west of the Jâma' a
sort of terrace (A) is added
(as is usual in the ancient
mosques of the Haurân).
This is built up with columns
and large hewn stones, and
the whole forms a stairway.
The remains of the Jâma'
show fragments of ancient
building stones and also
mosaics, with other carved
designs.

The pillars are covered
with Bedawîn tribe-marks
(" Wasm ") ; they were mostly the Tawâka
(٩١ الطواقة), the Wasm of the 'Ashîret ibn Fâiz
(عشيرة ابن فائيز), a branch tribe of the Beni
Sakher ; the marks called El-Maghzal (المغزل)

the Wasm of the 'Akama (عكمة ?), a branch tribe of Ej Ja'bna (الجعبنة and El-Ehlâl (الهلال) (or Halâl), the mark of the El-Ejbûr tribe (الجبور) were also found. These Wasms prove that these tribes once levied the Khuwwât (Brotherhood tax) upon Beit Râs and its vicinity.

Close up to the Jâma', to the east, are the remains of a church. Some other buildings, especially vaults, which were doubtless added at a later period, have destroyed its original character, but some of the foundation walls can still be distinctly traced.

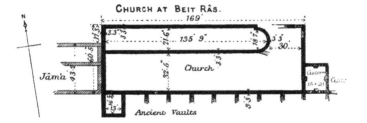

CHURCH AT BEIT RÂS.

The original length of the church from east to west must have been about 169 feet; its exact width cannot now be determined. An eastern apse is found in the northern nave, the diameter being 18 feet 7 inches. The Sheikh of Beit Râs, Mohammed El-Matlak, whose present dwelling-house is the ruin of the church and its vaults, and who has turned the apse into a barn for his cattle, states that he at one time dug out many marble slabs from the floor of this apse, with which material it was presumably paved.

Among the remains which he had left unbroken, I discovered a curious perforated stone, most likely at one time used for a font, which was now leaning against the north wall of the northern nave. It is carefully worked, being of a hard, white limestone, and measures 3 feet 3 inches square, and 2 feet wide.

FONT IN CHURCH, BEIT RÂS.

In the nave of the church, but not *in situ*, are two column capitals of limestone.

These capitals are apparently of the Byzantine style, and it is not improbable that the church dates from the era of the Byzantine occupation of the Decapolis.

At the eastern end of the church is a small

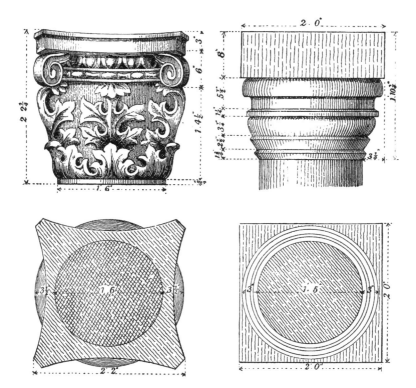

square cistern, divided into two parts by a circular
vault, which still holds water.

The whole plateau within the wall of the ancient
city is covered with great heaps of remains and
fragments of columns ; but the ruins are still more
weather-worn and defaced than are those already

L

described at Umm Keis, for the building material
used at Beit Râs is, as a rule, the crumbling-
limestone.   To the south of the site, and near
the city wall, is a large water basin, measuring
183 feet from north to south, and 131 feet from
west to east, with a depth of 26 feet; it is

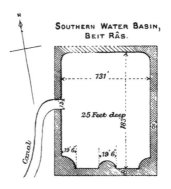

surrounded by a wall, laid in mortar, 8 feet in thickness.   The corners of the wall on the south, being
near a slope of the ground, are strengthened by projecting masonry; the northern wall is now falling
to ruin, though in winter the basin still fulfils its
original purpose of storing water.   In the western
wall is an arched opening, recently shut up, but
which proved on examination to have led into a
channel which connected this basin with an im-
mensely long cistern, which in size and appearance
is far superior to any found in other parts of this province.   In the upper part it is round, but is square

below, and from 11 feet 6 inches to 14 feet 8 inches wide, and 23 feet 8 inches high, hewn out of the solid limestone rock, and plastered with a yellow cement about $4\frac{1}{2}$ inches thick. This cistern in its length follows the slope of the Tell el-Khudr, from near

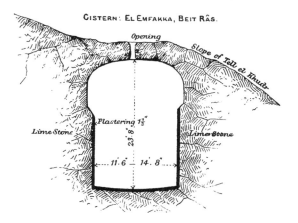

CISTERN: EL EMFAKKA, BEIT RÂS.

the southern basin to a point immediately north of El-Khudr; this end is now totally fallen to ruin and is open to the sky. Its entire length thus measures over 900 feet, and it was a reservoir of water sufficient to supply a large city; this cistern is called El-Emfakka, "the place hollowed out," by the natives, and is subdivided into small and large compartments by hollow walls, having a width of 3 feet 7 inches. The plastering, $4\frac{1}{2}$ inches thick, is composed of 7 or 8 different layers, each layer being still hard as stone. Over each compartment is a square hole in the roof, about 3 feet wide, evidently to allow of the drawing out of the water. Parts of this great cistern are now fallen to ruin, but parts are still well preserved and contain water in the winter season. The holes in the interior walls are occupied by thousands of crows and wild pigeons, also by hawks and bats; the flooring is covered with *débris* and mud, with pieces of broken jars. Some of this pottery is very ancient, being coloured with a sepia brown pigment, and is upwards of half an inch thick.

At the most conspicuous point on Tell el-Khudr, and at the centre of the small plateau, stands a columned building; here six basalt columns still project several feet out of the ground, and a numher of column shafts with Corinthian capitals and Attic bases (all of basalt) are found lying about the neighbourhood. The six columns are placed in the following order :—

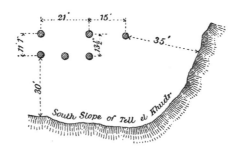

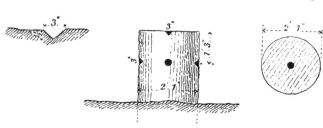

Each column has a diameter of 2 feet 1 inch, and shows dowel holes at the ends; also other holes occur on the shafts. The width of the dowel holes is 3 inches; they are conical and only 1½ inch deep.

At the western end of the plateau is a second birket or water basin, 125 feet long from north to south, 77 feet broad from east to west, and 26 feet deep. It is hewn out of the rock. Its south-western end was connected with a large cistern of rectangular shape, 77 feet long, 21 feet wide, and 15 feet deep. Both reservoirs are well plastered, the smaller one is now inhabited by the natives, and although it has but one opening, is the best residence to be found at Beit Râs. The walls of the large basin are 3 feet thick. To the east stands a wall, 3 feet 6 inches thick, and 21 feet further to the eastward a second wall, also 3 feet 6 inches thick, has been built. These walls are extremely well masoned, the large stones are carefully hewn, and they must

have formed part of an official building of some
sort.

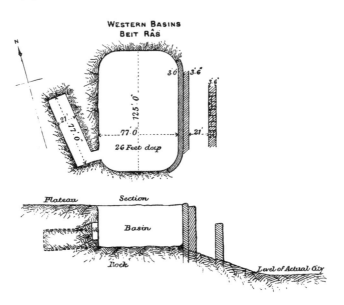

Outside the city wall, to the east, some other
large cisterns exist. Among these is the Bîr
Abu'l 'Umdân, so called on account of the two
columns which are laid across its mouth; it has a
depth of 31 feet. Of similar character is another
pit, the Bîr Umm el-Ghuzlân, and finally, further
eastward again, near the road to Maru, we find the
Birket Sôkarân, a rectangular tank measuring
136 feet by 84 feet, now in a total state of ruin.
Near it are several cisterns and other ruins.

The Tell el-Milh to the north has on it remains of ancient character, and is said to form part of the ancient site, for, according to tradition a "mighty castle" existed here. Of little importance, that is as regards its present remains, is the Khirbet el-Mîdân, lying a little to the south-east of Beit Râs, on a hill, where is also seen the Mohammedan Weli of Sîdna ed-Damari. The slopes and hills round Beit Râs show many caves and cisterns, but these are almost all now fallen in.

To judge from the ruins still to be seen, Beit Râs must have been a place of much importance in ancient times. Although its remains are not so imposing as those of Umm Keis, the care taken for the water supply, and the grand scale on which the ancient tanks were constructed, are a sufficient proof of its former greatness and wealth.

Beit Râs (not Beit er Râs) "the house of a head," or "of a chieftain," would answer perfectly to the conditions required for the site of the ancient Capitolias, and I am inclined to recall what I wrote in "Across the Jordan" (pages 240 and 241), where it was suggested that Zeizûn might represent this lost site. I have been led to this conclusion after fully exploring Beit Râs, and, above all, after standing on the plateau of Tell el-Khudr, and noting the view which embraces the whole country of the Decapolis. In addition, the

name Beit Râs is an almost literal Arabic transla-
tion of the Roman " Capitolias."

Kefr Yûba (1,730 feet above the sea).—A large
and populous village situated in a valley surrounded by ranges of fertile hills. It contains 110
houses and huts built of stone and mud, some of
them well masoned, and has a population of 600
souls. It is, therefore, nearly as large as Irbid.

To the south-west of the village, the predecessor
of the present Sheikh, Mahmûd el-'As'ad, built a
" Kasr," or Castle. This building may at first have
had the effect of awing the population of the neighbourhood, but at the present day it has nothing in
common with a castle but its name. It is a large
building, flanked by two tower-like wings, with walls
of 2 feet 3 inches thick, and, although not old, is
already fallen to decay. My adventures with Sheikh
Mahmûd have already been recorded in Chapter I
(*see* above, page 33), and it is to be hoped that his
insolence to foreigners will in future be curbed.
This large village has no other water supply than
that derived from ancient cisterns ; there is,
however, a Birket or pool to water the cattle on
the south of the town. The soil is good ; some
tobacco plantations are seen, also some olive trees
and vegetable gardens. Of ancient ruins I discovered little. Some Roman remains are built
into the wall of the " Kasr." A little to the west

of the village, however, I found a stone circle built with huge blocks, 43 feet in diameter, crowning the summit of a small hill. In the interior of the circle were the remains of a building. The inhabitants could or would give me no name for this relic of antiquity, although they doubtless have some denomination in use to call it by.

Jelameh and Tell Kefr Yûba are evidently very ancient sites, though they show but few and unimportant remains. To the east of Kefr Yûba several Mohammedan shrines or Welis exist, but they are all now in a state of ruin.

More interesting than these ruins of buildings are the Dolmens found extending to the north and to the south from the neighbourhood of Kefr Yûba up as far as Jumha. On the slopes and on the shoulders of the hills is a large field of these interesting monuments. Like the Dolmens of Jaulân the specimens here found stand, as a rule, on a terraced foundation of circular shape. This terrace consists of either (Fig. *a*) a single row of huge stones ; or (Fig. *b*) of two rows built up like a step ; or (Fig. *c*) of three or more rows built up one above the other to a height of 3 feet 3 inches without steps. Some Dolmens also were found without any terrace at all, as shown in Fig. *d*.

The foundations are all more or less of circular shape, but, as a rule, the Dolmen does not stand

Fig. a.

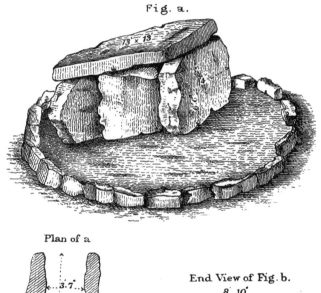

Plan of a

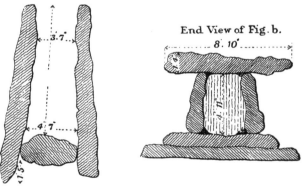

End View of Fig. b.

in its centre, the surrounding platform extending southwards and westwards to include about double the space of what is found on the north and east (*see*

Fig. b.

Fig. *c*, on page 172). This eccentric position is characteristic of these Dolmens, and was observed to exist in almost all cases. The covering slab forms a roof over the entire Dolmen, and covers the

Fig. c

side stones also, being of the hugest dimensions. On some of these covering slabs depressions, as

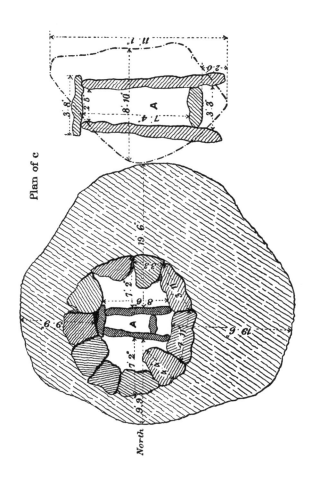

Plan of c

shown in Fig. *d*, p. 175, were observed, but it is
impossible to state whether they are artifically cut

Fig. c.

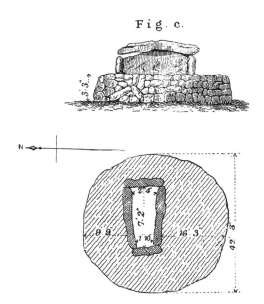

or merely a natural formation. The long side
stones are not set parallel, but give a cone-shaped
plan, the eastern end being narrower than the
western. The main axis of the Dolmens, as a
rule, ran east and west; some few, however, lay
north-west to south-east. In the greater number
of specimens the interior is closed by two small
end stones; in some there is one stone only at
the western end, the eastern being left open. But

I believe that in these instances the slab of stone,

DOLMEN NEAR KEFR YÛBA.
Fig. c.

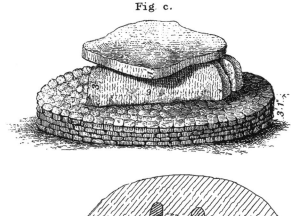

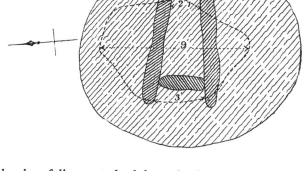

having fallen out, had been broken up or carried away. The kind of stone used is a hard limestone and the slabs were evidently split out, or found in their present forms and brought from the slopes of Wâd Samû'a, near Bersînia.

The distance between the Dolmens is not

DOLMEN NEAR KEFR YÛBA.
Fig. d.

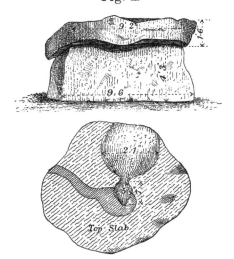

always the same, but generally measures from

Fig. d.

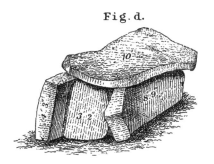

24 to 30 feet, and this space is often occupied

by the huge walls, generally formed of two parallel row of stones set 3 feet 3 inches apart and of a height of 2 feet 7 inches, which run for the most part tolerably exact, from north to south or from east to west. It is possible that these rows of stones may be the remains of the avenues. No ornamentation of the top slabs of the Dolmens, or holes in the end slabs (as was the case in Jaulân), were discovered here. I took occasion to open several specimens, by throwing down the covering and end slabs, in order to explore the interior of the Dolmen. After clearing away to a depth of about 14 inches of ordinary earth, a mass, consisting of ashes mixed with small pieces of burned coal, was discovered, with what were undoubtedly the remains of decayed bones, now nearly fallen to dust. Among the charred remains were several copper rings, 3 inches in diameter. These rings of copper (not brass, as erroneously stated in my reply in the October number, 1886, of the *Quarterly Statement*) showed a primitive ornamentation engraved round part of the outside, consisting of a zigzag pattern. Below the mass of charred remains a stone slab was always found, varying as to size, and beside it smaller stones had been set to fill out the space covered by the Dolmen. Below this slab the bare rock occurred.

These discoveries are of interest for elucidating

the question of what purpose Dolmens were built to serve. The number of Dolmens found near Kefr Yûba must have amounted to from 800 to 1,000, the specimens I explored numbering over a hundred.

'Ain en-Nakkâta.—A small spring near Tell el-Milh ; it generally runs dry in summer.

'Ard el-Karm.— A hillock near Dabûlia.

'Ard es-Stâwia.—A fertile tract of country lying between the hills, north-east of Beit Râs.

Abân.—A small ruin on the Wâd el-Ghafr.

Birket er-Rashâd.—A slope and mountain shoulder lying north of Bersînia ; covered by the Dolmen field.

Dabûlia.—A ruin near Beit Râs ; scattered stones and many cisterns and caves occur in the neighbourhood.

Jiyât Dabûlia.—A stony tract of land near Dabûlia.

El-Medâhel.—A strong position on the western slope of Tell el-Khudr.

El-Murûsh.—A field near the above.

El-Bâriha.—A village of 60 huts, containing a population of 300 souls, built in two quarters. The village is prosperous, and has excellent soil round it. The Sheikh's dwelling is a well-masoned building. In the courtyard are several sarcophagi of basalt, with a defaced ornamentation of heads.

M

A few limestone columns, of 1 foot 3 inches diameter and square capitals, were found lying near. No spring of water exists, but large and ancient cisterns are used for the storage of the rains.

The whole region between El-Bâriha and Irbid, which lies about a mile distant, is covered with ancient remains and traces of buildings. According to tradition the two towns were formerly included in one. Several cisterns, an ancient cemetery, and heaps of building stones border the road running between the two. El-Bâriha is, however, quite a modern village.

El-'Eber.—A mountain shoulder opposite Bersînia.

El-Bukâ'a.—The fertile plain lying east of Irbid, and extending to the Ez Zuweit hills, near Haurân.

Hakama.—A tolerably well-built village, containing 40 huts, and a population of 200 souls. Few ancient remains are found.

Jumha. — A poor-looking village of 35 huts, built of mud and stones, and having a population of 150 souls. A Birket (or Pool) occurs in the centre of the village, filled with muddy rain-water. The cisterns here are also extremely dirty. Some tobacco and vegetable gardens surround the village. Some ancient building stone, and some caves with loculi, lie near the Dolmen field on the hill to the east; and this was probably the old site.

Kefr Jâiz.—A moderate-sized village of 30 huts, and a population of 150 souls. The soil is poor. Some traces of ancient buildings exist and stones were found lying about.

Khirbet el-Mîdân.—An ancient site near Beit Râs, with caves and cisterns, and traces of old buildings.

Khirbet el-Butm.—An ancient site covering a small hill; with cisterns cut in the rock near it.

Kasr Wâd el-Ghafr.—A watch-tower in the Wâd el-Ghafr, near Irbid. The tower, 16 feet 5 inches square is now in a state of ruin, but is built of large stones. It protected a point of the great Haurân road where the traveller passes through a deep valley.

Maru.—A well-built village of 45 huts, with a population of about 230 souls. Sheikh 'Eisa en-N'amân is a Mohammedan Saint, whose tomb lies near the village, and is kept in excellent order. The ancient site extends southwards, but was not completely explored by me.

Rujm ed-Deiri.—A small hill ruin near Maru.

Srîs.—A small ruin on the Wâdy 'Ezz.

Tukbul.—A miserable village, containing some 40 huts, half of which are occupied by a population of about 80 souls. The soil is poor, and the country round stony. Among the rocks near, sarcophagi and cisterns occur. Large ancient building stones are also seen, and to the south of the village are the remains of the Makâm el-Arba'în (the Station of the Forty), now a ruin and nearly level with the earth. The prosperity of a village is easily judged by the condition of its Weli, or neighbouring shrine. If the village is flourishing, the Weli is regularly whitewashed, and the elders hold their meetings in its yard, first to pray, and then to talk and rest. If the village is going to ruin the Weli is neglected, and the elders meet on the summit of the village dung-heap, which then becomes their place of assembly.

Tell es-Sahn.—A small hill near Beit Râs.

Tell el-Butm.—A hill lying north-west of Beit Râs.

Tell Abu Zeita.—A hill bordering the Wâd el-Ghafr.

Tell esh-Shâ'ir.—The "Hill of the Poet;" a large mound lying north of Kefr Yûba, and bordering the Dolmen field on the north-east. I unfortunately was unable to visit its summit, which, according to the natives, has some ruins on it.

Tell Kefr Yûba.—The ancient site of the village of Kefr Yûba. Its remains cover a considerable area, but show no important remains.

Wâd Delham.—A small rocky and dry gorge, which joins the Wâl el-Ghafr, south of Tukbul.

Wâdy 'Ezz.—A gorge rising near Beit Râs and running into the above. It is dry in summer.

Wâd el-Ghafr.—This large and important wâdy is said to rise at a place five miles south-east of the limits of the present Map, near a place called Hôfa. It is the most important tributary of the Wâd el-'Arab, and contains much water in the winter time.

Wâd el-Mahwara, also called *Wâd Shômar.*—A large, deep, and dry gorge.

Wâd Kefr 'Ân.—A small and dry gorge joining the above near Kefr 'Ân.

Zebda (near Irbid).—A small village on a mountain ridge, containing 30 poor-looking huts and a population of under 120 souls.

Zahar en-Nasâra ("of the Christians").—A small village of 30 huts and a population of 120 souls. Its huts are built with stone and mud. The village is situated on the main road, and must have been a wealthy place of old ; it was inhabited in former days almost exclusively by Christians, as the name, En Nasâra, implies. It lies on the limits of western Beni Juhma District.

CHAPTER VII.

THE DISTRICT OR NÂHIYET OF EL-KÛRA.

THE Nâhiyet of el-Kûra is bounded on the north by the Wâd of Taiyibeh, also called the Wâd Samû'a. Its other limits lie outside the present Map, and only its northern part was surveyed. A small tract of land, occupying the shoulder between the Wâd Samû'a and the Wâd el-Hummâm (Wâd el-Tibn), belongs to the plateau of Northern 'Ajlûn ; but from the Wâd el-Tibn southwards the country rapidly rises towards the highlands of the Jebel 'Ajlûn. This part of the country is well wooded, and oak forests are found here even finer than those of Northern 'Ajlûn. Springs occur now and then along the wâdies.

Ayûn ej-Jurun.—Several springs in the deep valley of the Wâd el-Hummâm. The clear and good water of moderate supply, forms a small brook which flows down the wâdy and waters a couple of vegetable gardens, cultivated by an old Fellâh who lives in a little mud hut near them.

'Ayûn el-Hummâm. — Four springs, with a moderate supply of good water, lying east of the former. A little brook flows from them down the wâdy bed, but soon loses itself among the boulders. Several caves are seen in the cliff above these springs, but they are inaccessible without the aid of a ladder. Scattered ancient building stones lie round the springs, and some wild fig trees grow near.

Ain Amîri.—A spring to the south of the village of Jenîn, with a moderate supply of good water.

Abu Shûshy.—A tract of land lying north of Jenîn.

Benât el-Yusûr.—A group of beautiful Mallûl oaks, surrounding a fallen Weli (shrine) near Izmâl.

Dhaher Izmâl.—A mountain shoulder near the village of that name.

Es Sibia.—A small ruin surrounded by a woody country. There are near it some fallen caves and scattered building stones.

El Mâssia.—A hill slope south of Izmâl.

Izmâl.—A village of 30 huts, some of mud, some of stone, having a population of about 150 souls. Some olive and fig trees occur near, and extensive onion plantations, of which the people of this country are very fond. Izmâl has no spring, the water supply coming from the storage in the ancient cisterns. Some caves and remains of building material are seen near. It is now a poor village, the former name of which is said to have been "Kenz el-Mal" (the Treasury of Wealth). The Sheikh pretends that large caves were formerly discovered and opened here, and treasures taken from them in former centuries. The ancient site extends westwards of the present village.

Jenîn.—A village of 38 huts, built with but little care and of a very poor appearance. The population numbers 160 souls. Some old olives and groves of fig-trees are found in the neighbourhood. The soil is poor but the country is well wooded. To the north of the village is a group of fine Mallûl oaks, called the Shejarât el-Mustarîhi, with the remains of a Weli (or shrine) near them. The spring of 'Ain Amîri, to the south of the village, provides good water, though of moderate supply. Old cisterns and rock-cut sarcophagi and some few other ancient remains, with building stones, are found in the neighbourhood.

Karm el-Hummâm.—A hill slope west of Es Sibia.

Kefr Kîfia.—A ruin with scattered stones lying in a thickly-wooded region.

Sahel Jenîn.—A small plateau south-west of Jenîn.

Samû'a.—The village is of moderate size,

but poverty stricken on account of the extortions of the Damascene usurers, who have ruined the Sheikh and his people, having left him, of all his former considerable property, nothing but a single cow. The village contains 45 carelessly built huts of stone and mud, and a population of about 180 souls. Its population is now rapidly decreasing, and many of the villagers have already left, though but a few years ago Samû'a was a flourishing town. Among the houses are many cisterns of large size, some of which, though not plastered, still hold rain-water. I measured one of these cisterns, near which some remarkable remains of ancient buildings were discovered, and found its diameter to be 35 feet 6 inches, and its depth 27 feet. The Sheikh assured me that it had originally a depth of over 60 feet, and that the villagers had for ten years back thrown all the refuse and ashes of the village into this cistern. Several ancient vaults in the interior of the village seem to be of Mohammedan architecture. While digging for building stones the Fellahîn have found subterranean caves containing rock-cut sarcophagi. The entire neighbourhood of Samû'a shows remains of ancient character, and it was evidently of old a site of considerable extent. The ruins and places in the immediate neighbourhood have the following names—Khirbet el-Kenûsi, El-Eber, El-Ghâba, El-Meshed, and Ehreinî. At the last-mentioned place, to the west of the village, are many tombs, and an ancient cemetery was discovered, with quantities of well-hewn building-stones. The remains, however, show no distinct character. Some olive trees and tobacco fields are cultivated near. To the north of Samû'a stands a beautiful Mallûl oak ; the spreading branches have a diameter of 99 feet, the trunk measures 3 feet 4 inches across, and its age is said to exceed 160 years. The branches and leaves are never broken off, it being considered a " Fakîri " (a Saint's tree). The southern neighbourhood of Samû'a shows many large stone slabs lying in disorder on the surface of the ground, as though there had been here a Dolmen field.

Tibneh.—2,013 feet above the sea. This is the principal village of the District of El-Kûra, but it could not be explored at the time of my visit. I was told that it has a population of more than 1,000 men, and extensive vineyards and olive-groves surround it, it being as important a place as Ed Dera'ah in Haurân: Its position on the mountain is very commanding, and a fine view must be had from its houses.

Weli Ja'far et-Taiyâr.—A fallen Mâkam (shrine) shaded by fine Mallûl oak trees.

Wâdy Fidel, or *Wâdy el-Birket.*—A gorge beginning near Izmâl ; it is dry in summer.

Wâdy el-Hummâm.—Only a small portion of this great wâdy is here mapped. Its upper part, below Tibneh, is called Wâd el-Tibn, further down, at the 'Ayûn el-Hummâm, it is called after these springs, and near its entrance into the Ghôr it again changes its name. The wâdy bed is covered with many large and small blocks of stone, and although in summer its upper part is nearly dry, in winter it is filled by a nearly unfordable torrent. The valley is wide and deep, and gentle slopes alternate along its banks with picturesque precipices.

Wâdy es Siklâb.—A tributary of the Wâd el-Hummâm. It rises near Sibia ; its upper part is dry, but near its junction the springs of 'Ayûn Siklâb gush out on the slopes and form a stream, sufficiently strong to work some corn mills. The name " Siklâb," Slavonian, is remarkable. Some men of that nation may have been settled near here in ancient times.

Wâd 'Ain es-Sinn.—A deep and narrow, but well-wooded, wâdy, which is a tributary of the Wâd el-Hummâm. It lies east of Tibneh, and contains a small brook.

Wâd el-Kruka.—A small dry gorge, rising at Samû'a, and joining the Wâd el-Hummâm.

Wâd Jenin, called also the *Wâd et-Taiyibeh,* the *Wâdy Samû'a,* or the *Wâdy es-Sheil.*—It forms the boundary between the Districts of El-Kûra and El-Wustîyeh. It is dry in summer, being wide, steep, and rocky. Neither the beginning nor the termination of this wâdy could be surveyed, and merely a part of its course is given in the present Map.

KADA TABARIYA.

The above are the villages, sites, and names found in the Kada Irbid, as far as the region is mapped at present. There remain to mention some few names belonging to the Province of Kada Tabarîya (Tiberias) which lie in the country of the Ghôr, or Jordan Valley.

'Arâk Abu Yedeiyeh.—The slopes of the Sharî'at el-Menâdireh, bordering the river on its course through the Ghôr where the Sharî'a, or Yarmûk, has cut for itself a deep bed in the alluvial soil of the Ghôr.

Ed Delhemiyeh.—This village (which is also given on the Map of Western Palestine) has at the present day 55 huts, built of mud and the ancient stones brought from the opposite site of El-Melhamîyeh, also called El-Bekâ by the Bedawîn. The population numbers 250 souls. The two owners of the place, one a native of Tiberias and the other Khuweitîn Aga, Sheikh of the Arab Sukhûr el-Ghôr (*see* above, p. 86), have settled the Bedawîn of this tribe here, and they now cultivate the rich soil of this section of the Jordan Valley. El-Melhamîyeh lies opposite the village, west and across the Jordan. It is a site showing remains of buildings, and some scattered stones. The hill on which Ed Delhemiyeh is built appears to be of artificial construction.

El-Adeisîyeh.—A small village in the northern Ghôr, built of miserable-looking huts. The place is generally abandoned in summer by the tribe of the Arab Sukhûr el-Ghôr, who number about 50 souls. Irrigated lands and vegetable gardens are found here, for the soil is most fertile.

Es Shûni.—A small village in the Ghôr, near the Wâd el-'Arab. Its 15 huts and grain stores are well built, with stone and mortar. The 60 inhabitants are partly of the Sukhûr el-Ghôr tribe, partly immigrants from the Lebanon Districts brought here by the energetic Kaimakâm (or Governor) of Tiberias, who wishes to cultivate the soil of the Ghôr, and raise cotton and sugarcane here as in former times. Opposite the village, which is situated on an elevated tract below Tell el-Muntâr, some Bedawîn have erected some wretched mud huts.   The Wâd el-'Arab here runs with a fine stream, and is used to water the newly-planted gardens.   If well attended to Esh Shûni will soon become a most flourishing place. At the point near here, where the great Haurân road crosses the Wâd el-'Arab, there are ruins of a small but ancient bridge.   Esh Shûni was an ancient site, and, owing to its situation at the point of junction of two great high roads, must have been, in old times, an important place.

Ma'âd.—A village of 35 tolerably well-built huts, lying on the slopes of 'Ajlûn.   The population numbers 140 souls.

The Weli esh-Sheikh Ma'ad is a carefully-guarded tomb, which is whitewashed and cleaned with great zeal by the inhabitants of the village. The great Haurân road passes near the village. The ancient remains existing here were not thoroughly explored.

THE END

INDEX TO THE NAMES.

———o———

Transliteration.	Arabic.	Translation.	Page.
'Ain Haîyeh	عين حية	Snake Spring.	84
'Ain Kasaksobeh	عين قصقصوبة		85
'Ain el Kirkâsi	عين القرقاسة		127
'Ain el Kusab	عين القصب	Of the Reed	83
'Ain Mendah	عين مندح		127
'Ain Mkeis (or Umm Keis)	عين مكيس		84
'Ain en Nakkâta	عين النقاطة	Of the Dropping	177
'Ain Ra'ân	عين رعان	Of the Mountain-spurs	83
'Ain es Sahn	عين الصحن	Of the Dish	83
'Ain Samar	عين سمر	The Brown Spring	115
'Ain es Smeirât	عين السميرات	Of the Thorn-bush	84, 126
'Ain es Sukkar	عين السكر	Of the Sugar (Mill)	84
'Ain et Turâb	عين التراب	Of the Earth, Soil	84
'Ain Umm ej Jrein	عين ام الجرين	Of the Little Trough	84
'Ain Umm el Kharâk	عين ام الخرق	That has pierced its way	84
'Ain Wonsa	عين ونسة		85
El 'Ajami	العجمي	(The Stranger)	94
Akhfas el Heitalîyeh	اخفس الحيطلية	The Little Eye of the Heitalîyeh	114
'Arab el 'Abîd	عرب العبيد	The 'Abîd Bedouins	38, 86
'Arab el Mukhaibeh	عرب المخيدبة		87
'Arab Sukhûr el Ghôr	عرب صخور الغور		85
'Arab Sukhûr el 'Alâ	عرب صخور العلا		125

Transliteration.	Arabic.	Translation.	Page.
'Arâk Abu Yedeiyeh	عراق ابو يدية	The Cliff of the Little Hand	188
'Arâk el Heitalîyeh	عراق الحيطلية	The Cliff of the Slopes	114
'Arâk er Râhib	عراق الراهب	Of the Monk	126
'Arâk ez Zutt	عراق الزط	Of the Murmuring	126
'Arakîb el Eshshi	عرقيب العشة	The Rocky Slopes of the Nest	115
'Arâkîb es Sâkhui	عرقيب الساخنة	The Rocky Slopes of the Sick Man	126
Arbela of the Decapolis (Irbid)			154
Ard el 'Alâ	ارض العلا	The Ground or Plain of the Height	88
Ard el Burz	ارض البرز	Of the Isthmus	88
Ard el Ghanj	ارض الغنج	Of the Treasure	125
Ard el Karm	ارض الكرم	Of the Vineyard	177
Ard el Mahajjeh	ارض المحجة	Of the Wide Road	125
Ard el Musheirfi	ارض المشيرفة		125
Ard el 'Seidûr	ارض الصيدور	The Watershed of a Valley	125
Ard es Stâwia	ارض الستاوية		177
'Arkûb ed Dweirîkh	عرقوب الدويريخ	The Stony Slope of Ed Dweirîkh	87
Arkûb el Emessakhîn	عرقوب المساخين	The Changed Rocks	126
'Arkûb el Fakîri	عرقوب الفقيرة	Of the Fakir's Tree	87
'Arkûb el Hummad	عرقوب الحماض	Of the Sorrel Bush	125
'Arkûb ej Jûk	عرقوب الجوق	Of the Broad Neck	87

N

Transliteration.	Arabic.	Translation.	Page.
'Arkûb Mkeis (or Umm Keis)	عرقوب مكيس		87
'Arkûb Rûmi	عرقوب رومه	Of the Quiver	87
'Arkûb Umm Tûd	عرقوب أم طود	Of the Mountain Ridge	87
'Arûk ej Jenânîyeh	عروق الجنانية	The Water Course of the Garden	87
'Ayûn ej Jurun	عيون الخرن	The Springs of the Trough	182
'Ayûn el Hummâm	عيون الحمام	Of the Bath	183
El Bâriha	البارحة	Of Yesterday	177
Bayâdet 'Ulûka	بياضة علوقة	The Limestone Slope of the Pasture	89
Beit Râs (Capitolias)	بيت راس	The Chief's House	154–168
Benât el Yusûr	بنات اليسر	The Daughters of the Right Hand	183
Bersînia	برسينيا		127–129
Bîr Abu-l 'Umdân	بير ابو العمدان	The Cistern of the Columns	166
Bîr Umm el Ghazlân	بير ام الغزلان	The Cistern of the Gazelles	166
El Birket	البركة	The Pool	75
Birket el 'Arâis or Birket el Tawâka	بركة العرائس بركة الطواقة	The Brides' Pool, or The Pool of the Caves	88
Birket er Rashâd	بركة الرشاد		177
Birket Sôkarân	بركة سوكران		166
El Bukâ'a	البقعة	The Depressed Plain	178

Transliteration.	Arabic.	Translation.	Page.
El Ehsûn or El Ekseir	الحصون , القصير	The Castles	115
El Eklâ'a el Mutraki-bât	القلع المتركبات	The Piled-up Rocks	131
El Emfakka	المفقئه	The Hollow	163
El 'Eshshi	العشة	The Nest	116
El Fakhed	الفخد	The Thigh	93
Freika'	قريقة	The Hopper	135
El Fu'ara	الفعرة	The Roarer	97
El Ghâba	الغابة	The Low-ground	186
Hakama	حكمة	Medicine	178
El Halfawîyeh	الحلفوية	The Field of Rushes	131
Halîbna	حليبنا		117
Hammet Rîh el Ghanam	حمة ريح الغنم	The Hot Bath of the Sheep-sickness	91
Hammet esh Sheikh	حمة الشيخ	The Sheikh's Bath	91
El Hammi (or El Hammeh)	الحمة	The Hot Bath	91
El Hareit	الحريث	The Arable Field	93
Hâtim	حاتم	The Obligation	98–101
El Hâwiyân or Hâwit el 'Alu	الحاويان حاوية العلو	The Rocks or The High Rock	92
Hawwar	حوّر	Whitened	98
El Heitalîyeh	الحيطلية		116
Helâl el 'Ulleika	حلال العليقة	The Field of Raspberries	117

Transliteration.	Arabic.	Translation.	Page.
Khallet Sbeih	خلة صبيح	The Lovely Dale	138
Khallet et Tahtaniya	خلة التحتنية	The Lower Dell	103
Kharâj	خراج		137
Khirbet el 'Askalâni	خربة العسقلانى	The Ruin of the Ascalonite	136
Khirbet el Bueiri	خربة البويرة	Of the Little Ruin	136
Khirbet el Bueiri Seidûr	خربة البويرة صيدور		136
Khirbet el Butm	خربة البطمة	Of the Terebinth	179
Khirbet ed Deir	خربة الدير	Of the Convent	117
Khirbet Ekseir Fu'ara	خربة قصير فعرة	Of Fu'ara's Rocks, or Castle	102
Khirbet Ekseir Hâtim	خربة قصير حاتم	Of Hâtim's Rocks, or Castle	102
Khirbet Hasân	خربة حسان		136
Khirbet Jeharra	خربة جحرا	Of the Hidden One	102
Khirbet el Kenûsi	خربة القنوسة	Of the Summit	186
Khirbet Mâkûk	خربة مافوق		101
Khirbet el Mîdân	خربة الميدان	Of the Race-course	167, 179
Khirbet el Mikyal	خربة المقيل		102
Khirbet es Sâkhni	خربة الساخنة	Of the Sick	136
Khirbet et Tabak	خربة الطبق	Of the Terrace	101
El Khneizîr	الخنديزير	The Little Pig	93
El Khudr	الخضر	The Green Man	155
Kôba	قبع	Hedgehog	137
Kumeim	قميم	The Little Summit	137

* Probably a mistake for المشهد, el-Mesh-hed, The Place of Martyrdom.—ED.

Transliteration.	Arabic.	Translation.	Page.
Tâhûnet el 'Arîd	طاحونة العريض	Of the Broad Place	143
Tâhûnet el 'Azzâm	طاحونة عزام		143
Tâhûnet el Beshâiri	طاحونة البشايرة		143
Tâhûnet ed Dueikât	طاحونة الدويكات		143
Tâhûnet el Emheidât	طاحونة الامهيدات	Of the Terrace	143
Tâhûnet el Ersân	طاحونة الارسان	Of the Halters	143
Tâhûnet el Klei'ât	طاحونة القليعات	Of the Little Castles or Rocks	143
Tâhûnet Matlak el Ahsein	طاحونة مطلق الحصين		143
Tâhûnet Mazeid Ef-fendi	طاحونة مزيد افندى		143
Tâhûnet el Menshîyeh	طاحونة المنشية	The Productive Mill	143
Tâhûnet el Messadîn	طاحونة المسدين	Of the Poor Saints	143
Tâhûnet Sa'ûd 'Azzâm	طاحونة سعود عزام		143
Tâhûnet Umm Dâlieh	طاحونة ام دالية	Of the Vine Tendril	143
Tâket el 'Alu	طاقة العلو	The Terrace of the Height	107
Et Taiyibeh	الطيبة	The Good	123
Tell Abu Zeita	تل أبو زيتا	Olive-tree Hill	180
Tell el Butm	تل البطم	Of the Terebinth	180
Tell ed Deîr	تل الدير	Of the Convent	130
Tell el Kâk	تل القاق	Of the Crow	143
Tell Kefr Yûba	تل كفر يوبا		180
Tell el Khudr	تل الخضر	Of the Green Man	154
Tell el Milh	تل الملح	Of Salt	167

Transliteration.	Arabic.	Translation.	Page.
Tell el Muntâr	تل المنطار	Of the Watch Tower	107
Tell es Sahn	تل الصحن	Of the Dish	180
Tell es Seirawân	تل السيروان		143
Tell esh Shâ'ir	تل الشاعر	Of the Poet	180
Tell Zara'a	تل زرعة	Of the Cultivated Land	142
Tibneh	تبنة	Straw-stem	186
Tukbul	تقبل		179
Umm Erkâ'a	ام رقاع	The Place of the Target	144
Umm el Ghuzlân	ام الغزلان	The Place of Gazelles	144
Umm Hanna	ام حنا	The Mother of Hannâ	144
Umm Keis (or Mkeis)	ام كيس		46–79
Umm el Khawâbi	ام الخوابى	The Place of Relationships	108
Umm en Nakhla	ام النخلة	The Place of the Palm-tree	108
Wâd, or Wâdy Abu Dmeikh	وادي أبو دميخ		112
Wâd Abu Sarâj	وادي أبو سراج	Of the Saddles	146
Wâd el 'Ain	وادي العين	Of the Spring	113
Wâd 'Ain 'Atiyeh	وادي عين عطية	Spring of the Gift	113
Wâd 'Ain el Mallâki	وادي عين الملاقى		113
Wâd 'Ain es Sinn	وادي عين السن	Spring of the Tooth	187

Transliteration.	Arabic.	Translation.	Page.
Wâdy Kleit	وادي قليط	Of the Ford	117
Wâd el Kruka	وادي القرقة	Of the Hen	187
Wâd Kumeim	وادي قميم	Of the Dough-ladle	146
Wâd el Mahwara	وادي المحورة		181
Wâd Mâkûk	وادي ماقوق		112
Wâd Masa'ud	وادي مسعود	The Fortunate Valley	112
Wâd el Muntamri	وادي المنتمري		112
Wâd el 'Ora	وادي العورة	Of the Squint	118
Wâd Samar	وادي سمر	The Brown Valley	111
Wâd Sammâ	ودي صما		146
Wâdy Samu'a	وادي سموع		188
Wâd esh Shômar	وادي السومر		146
Wâdy es Siklâb	وادي السقلاب	Of the Slavonian	187
Wâd et Taiyibeh	وادي الطيبة		146, 188
Wâd el 'Ulleika	وادي العليقة	Of the Raspberry	118
Wâd Umm el Karein	وادي ام القرين	(vulgar) Of the Two Horns	118
Wâd Zahar	وادي زحر		145
Wâd Zebda	وادي زبدة	Of the Cream	146
Weli Ja'far et Taiyâr	ولى جعفر الطيار		186
Weli esh Sheikh Muhammed el Udamy	ولى الشيخ محمد العضمى		120
Weli esh Sheikh Sa'ad	ولى الشيخ سعد		152

Transliteration.	Arabic.	Translation.	Page.
Zahar el 'Akabi	زحر العقبة	Zahar of the Precipice	147
Zahar en Nasâra	زحر النصارا	Of the Christians	181
Zebda, of el-Wustîyeh	زبدة , زبدا		147
Zebda, of Irbid			181
Zikel	زقل	Thieves	113
Zôr el Heshra	زور الحشرة		118
Zôr el Kusseib	زور القصيب	The Lowland of the Reeds	113
Zôr en Nîs	زور النيس	Of the Monkey	118

HARRISON AND SONS, PRINTERS IN ORDINARY TO HER MAJESTY, ST. MARTIN'S LANE, LONDON.